D1245548

TRACING YOUR
NORTHERN IRISH
ANCESTORS

FAMILY HISTORY FROM PEN & SWORD

Tracing Your Yorkshire Ancestors
Rachel Bellerby

Tracing Your Royal Marine Ancestors
Richard Brooks and Matthew Little

Tracing Your Pauper Ancestors
Robert Burlison

Tracing Your Labour Movement Ancestors
Mark Crail

Tracing Your Army Ancestors
Simon Fowler

A Guide to Military History on the Internet
Simon Fowler

Tracing Your Northern Ancestors
Keith Gregson

Your Irish Ancestors
Ian Maxwell

Tracing Your Scottish Ancestors
Ian Maxwell

Tracing Your Air Force Ancestors
Phil Tomaselli

Tracing Your Secret Service Ancestors
Phil Tomaselli

Tracing Your Criminal Ancestors
Stephen Wade

Tracing Your Police Ancestors
Stephen Wade

Tracing Your Jewish Ancestors
Rosemary Wenzerul

Fishing and Fishermen
Martin Wilcox

TRACING YOUR NORTHERN IRISH ANCESTORS

Ian Maxwell

Pen & Sword
FAMILY HISTORY

First published in Great Britain in 2010
and reprinted in 2013 & 2014 by
PEN AND SWORD FAMILY HISTORY
An imprint of
Pen & Sword Books Ltd
47 Church Street
Barnsley, South Yorkshire
S70 2AS

ISBN 978 1 84884 167 3

Typeset in Palatino and Optima by
Phoenix Typesetting, Auldgirth, Dumfriesshire

Printed and bound in England
CPI Group (UK) Ltd, Croydon, CR0 4YY

Pen & Sword Books Ltd incorporates the Imprints of Aviation, Atlas,
Family History, Fiction, Maritime, Military, Discovery, Politics, History,
Archaeology, Select, Wharncliffe Local History, Wharncliffe True Crime,
Military Classics, Wharncliffe Transport, Leo Cooper, The Praetorian Press,
Remember When, Seaforth Publishing and Frontline Publishing.

For a complete list of Pen & Sword titles please contact
PEN & SWORD BOOKS LIMITED
47 Church Street, Barnsley, South Yorkshire, S70 2AS, England
E-mail: enquiries@pen-and-sword.co.uk
Website: www.pen-and-sword.co.uk

CONTENTS

Introduction		1
Chapter 1	*Where to Begin*	11
	What Do I Need to Know?	12
	A Walk Round a Graveyard	12
	Surnames	12
	Visiting the Archives	15
	Family History Centres	17
	Heritage or Genealogical Centres	17
	Societies	18
	DNA	18
Chapter 2	*Census Records*	20
	1821	20
	1831	20
	1841	21
	1851	21
	1861, 1871, 1881 and 1891	22
	1901	22
	1911	23
	1901 and 1911 Censuses Online	23
	Old-age Pension Claims	24
Chapter 3	*Civil Registration*	25
	Birth Certificates	26
	Marriage Certificates	26
	Death Certificates	27
	The Indexes	27
	General Register Office, Belfast, and	
	District Registrars' Offices	27
	Church of Latter-Day Saints	29
Chapter 4	*Eighteenth-century Records*	31
	Survey of Downpatrick, 1708	31
	Protestant Householders, 1740	31
	Householders Returns, 1766	31

	Armagh 'Census', 1770	32
	Flaxseed Premiums, 1796	33
	Catholic Migrants from Ulster, 1795–96	34
	Records Relating to the 1798 Rebellion	34
Chapter 5	Seventeenth-century Records	36
	1602 'Census of Fews'	36
	Fiants of the Tudor Sovereigns, 1521–1603	36
	Calendars of Patent Rolls from the Reigns of James I and Charles I	37
	Muster Rolls, 1630s and 1640s	37
	Depositions of 1641 Rising	40
	Books of Survey and Distribution	41
	Civil Survey of Ireland	42
	Census of Ireland, c. 1659	43
	Poll Tax Returns, 1660	44
	Hearth-money Rolls, 1666	45
	Subsidy Rolls, 1630s, 1660s	46
	The Franciscan Petition Lists, 1670–71	47
	Names of Those Attainted by James II, 1689	48
	Williamite War and Siege of Londonderry, 1689	49
	Regiments of Infantry	50
Chapter 6	The Plantation of Ulster	51
	The Records	55
	Plantation Records of the London Companies	56
Chapter 7	Church Records	59
	The Records	65
	Church of Ireland Records	65
	Indexes to Church Registers	67
	Roman Catholic Church Records	68
	Presbyterian Church Records	69
	Methodist Records	70
	The Religious Society of Friends (or Quakers)	71
	Congregational Church Records	71
	Baptist Church Records	72
	Non-Subscribing Presbyterian Church (or Unitarians)	72
	Reformed Presbyterian Church (or Covenanters)	73
	Moravian Church Records	73

	Huguenot Records	74
	Jewish Records	74
	Census Returns	75
	Marriage Licence Bonds	76
Chapter 8	School Records	78
	Secondary Education	84
	Third-level Education	85
Chapter 9	Valuation and Tithe Records	87
	Tithe Applotment Books, 1823–38	87
	Valuation Records	88
Chapter 10	Landed Estate Records	93
	The Name of the Local Landlord	98
	The Records	98
	Other Classes of Records	100
Chapter 11	Wills and Testamentary Records	107
	Wills Before 1858	108
	Wills, 1858–1900	109
	Wills From 1900	110
Chapter 12	Printed Sources	112
	Ordnance Survey Memoirs	112
	Street Directories and Almanacs	113
	Countrywide Directories	114
	Provincial Directories	115
	Newspapers	119
Chapter 13	Poor Law Records	122
	The Records	127
Chapter 14	Local-government Records	130
	Corporations	130
	Belfast Corporation	130
	Other Corporations	132
	Town Commissioners	133
	Grand Jury	134
	County Councils	136

Chapter 15 *Military Records*   138
  The Royal Irish Fusiliers Museum   139
  The Royal Inniskillen Fusiliers Regimental Museum   140
  The Regimental Museum of The Royal Ulster Rifles   140
  Militia   141
  Yeomanry   143
  Volunteers   145

Chapter 16 *Electoral Records*   147
  Voters, Poll and Freeholders' Records   147
  Poll Books   148
  Electoral Registers and Voters' Lists   149

Chapter 17 *Law and Order*   152
  Policing   152
  The Courts   154
  Crown and Peace Records   154

Chapter 18 *Emigration*   157
  Public Record Office of Northern Ireland, Belfast   159
  Ulster American Folk Park   162

Chapter 19 *Miscellaneous Collections*   164
  Solicitors' Collections   164
  Business Records   165
  Orange Order Records   166
  Hospital Collections   168
  Charity Records   169
  Pedigrees   170
  Ulster Covenant, 1912   171

Appendix: Useful Addresses   172
Bibliography and Sources   177
Index   179

To my sons Scott and Callum, without whose help this book would have been finished in half the time

.

INTRODUCTION

Northern Ireland was established as a distinct region within the United Kingdom on 3 May 1921 under the terms of the Government Ireland Act 1920. The new autonomous region was formed from six of the nine counties of Ulster, namely Armagh, Antrim, Down, Fermanagh, Londonderry and Tyrone. These were the counties with the highest concentration of Unionists who had opposed a series of Irish Home Rule bills designed to grant limited autonomy to a parliament in Dublin. The partition of Ireland, however, left a deep legacy of mistrust and division that often manifested itself as political unrest and violence until the beginning of the twenty-first century.

The Province's early history extends further back than written records and survives mainly in legends such as the Ulster Cycle. Before the arrival of the Celts during the second half of first millennium BC, Ulster was already sparsely inhabited by early migrants who had probably crossed the narrow sea from Scotland to the Antrim coast and gradually moved further south. They lived a primitive existence by hunting in the forests and fishing the streams and lakes. Next came the first farmers who used stone implements for felling trees and preparing the soil for grain and kept cattle, sheep and pigs. The Ulster landscape contains many examples of the tombs they left as monuments to their dead.

The first Celtic-speaking people appeared in Ireland during the Iron Age around 500 BC. These people, known to the Greeks as Keltoi or Celts, had dominated central and western Europe and spoke an Indo-European language, which would develop into the P-Celtic language of Britain and Gaul and Q-Celtic, the ancestor of Irish Gaelic. The Celts enjoyed the advantage of having weapons made of iron. They seem to have moved into Ireland directly from the continent, perhaps from northern Spain or western France, into the west and south of the county. Another wave probably came through Britain into north-east Ireland. The Celts would dominate much of Ireland for nearly a thousand years.

The historic period begins with the introduction of Christianity in the fifth century, and Ulster first emerges into the light in documents ascribed to St Patrick. Thereafter, it developed a highly literate society which has left us a substantial corpus of literature in both Latin and Irish. Using annals, genealogies, king lists and other sources we can assemble the names of the many peoples who dominated the island, the territories they held and the rise and fall of their various dynasties.

Much of Ulster's colourful early history has taken place in and around the ancient ecclesiastical settlement of Armagh. The name is the English version of the Irish Ard Macha – the Hill of Macha – the legendary queen who built her fortress about 600 BC on the hill around which the city would develop. More than 600 years later another queen of that name built the palace of Emain Macha a few miles from the city at the site now known as Navan Fort. It became the ancient seat of the Kings of Ulster. Archaeologists have discovered at Navan the traces of a giant temple, the largest prehistoric building in Britain, which was erected for the purpose of ritual destruction and burial beneath the mound that can be seen today. There was a royal settlement with an enclosure and archaeologists have unearthed ancient weapons, jewellery and the bones of people and animals, including the skull of a Barbary ape. Here too the legendary exploits of Cuchullain and the Red Branch Knights were preserved in the oral tradition. After the destruction of Navan, the centre of power moved to the present site of Armagh, probably in the fifth century AD. The abandonment of Emain Macha seems to be connected with the establishment of a very early church at Armagh by Patrick and his followers.

In early medieval Ireland, the Uí Néill (O'Neill) dynasty dominated Ulster from their base in Tír Eóghain (Eoghan's Country) – most of which forms modern County Tyrone. The Ó Domhnaill (O'Donnell) dynasty were Ulster's second most-powerful clan from the early thirteenth century through to the beginning of the seventeenth century. The O'Donnells ruled over Tír Chonaill (most of modern County Donegal) in west Ulster. After the Norman invasion of Ireland in the twelfth century, the east of the Province fell by conquest to Norman barons. In the North of Ireland, the Normans, led by a Somerset knight, John de Courcy, overthrew the over-kingdom of Ulaid and replaced it with the earldom of Ulster. He brought with him Flemish crossbowmen and Welsh long-bowmen, who would pour down a deadly rain of bolts and arrows long before the Irish could get within range to use their shortbows and hurl their lances. 'In this island,' Gerald of Wales wrote, 'as in every country, the people of the North are always more warlike and savage.' The Irish, he reported, fought without armour: 'They regard weapons as a burden, and they think it brave and honourable to fight unarmed . . . They are quicker and more expert than any other people in throwing, when everything fails, stones as missiles, and such stones do great damage to the enemy in an engagement'.

Antrim Tower, from the Handbook of Irish Antiquities, *William F Wakeman (1848).*

For a quarter of a century de Courcy ruled his Ulster lands with all the independence of a medieval warlord. He minted his own half-pennies and farthings and administered his own justice with the assistance of his seneschal, chamberlain and constable. By 1300, the Normans controlled most of the country. But they did not succeed in conquering Ireland as they had conquered England. Their task was more difficult in Ireland because there was no central government in the country which they could seize. Continuous warfare gradually reduced the strength of the Normans, and fresh settlers did not replace them. Those in remote areas began to adopt the language and customs of their Irish neighbours. This ensured that Ulster would remain the most Gaelic part of Ireland until the end of the sixteenth century. Until that point Ulster remained unaffected by the piecemeal conquest of the rest of Ireland. During the closing years of the reign of Queen Elizabeth I a protracted and bloody war took place with the native Irish forces scoring a succession of victories over the English armies. With the arrival of Lord Mountjoy as governor in 1600, the war began to turn in favour of the English Crown. By using a scorched earth policy, which included devastating south Armagh in Ulster, Mountjoy undermined the Irish forces. Hugh O'Neill, Earl of Tyrone and the chief general of the Irish forces, surrendered shortly after the accession of James I in 1603.

Hugh O'Neill signed the Treaty of Mellifont in 1603 and was allowed to retain his lands in Ulster. However, his position was undermined by the presence of English officials and by garrisons stationed throughout his territories. Therefore, in 1607, along with his family, retainers and fellow lords, he fled to the continent. Having reneged on their allegiance to the King, their lands were seized by the Crown and in January 1608 a plan, which called for the plantation of much of Ulster, was published. The subsequent Plantation included the counties of Tyrone, Donegal, Cavan, Fermanagh, Armagh and Coleraine. Down and Antrim already had sizable Scottish populations and were not included in the Plantation scheme.

The British 'undertakers' (principal landlords) were assigned the lands at favourable terms. Proportions allocated varied from 2,000, to 1,000 acres. Undertakers were expected to settle twenty-four British males per 1,000 acres of lands granted. On lands allocated to English and Scottish undertakers, the native Irish population was to be cleared off these estates, the principle of 'segregation' underpinning the settlement project. Stipulated building conditions were also scaled according to the size of the proportion granted. Thus, undertakers who were granted the largest proportions, 2,000 acres, were expected to build a castle on their lands, whereas stone bawns (walled fortifications) were required to be built by undertakers with smaller proportions. Building and settlement had to be completed within three years. Captain Nicholas Pynnar was commissioned in 1618 to examine every settlement in the Plantation. He found 'at least 8,000 Men of British Birth and Descent, to do his Majesty's Service for Defence thereof'. Since his figure names only fighting men, perhaps four times this number were then present in Ulster when those outside fighting age, women and children are taken into account.

An important part of the Plantation was the settlement of the county of Coleraine (now Londonderry) by the corporation of the city of London. Receiving a grant of practically the whole of the county the corporation undertook to spend £20,000, and within 2 years to build 200 houses in Derry and 100 in Coleraine. This was the most successful part of the settlement, and to it Londonderry owes its present name. New waves of migration occurred throughout the seventeenth century and by the 1640s, the Protestant population in Ulster had swelled to some 40,000. Sir William Brereton, an Englishman travelling through Ayrshire in 1634, wrote:

Above ten thousand persons have, within two last years past, left the country wherein they lived . . . and are gone for Ireland. They have come by one hundred in company through the town, and three hundred have gone on hence together, shipped for Ireland at one tide . . . Their swarming in Ireland is so much taken notice of and disliked, as that the Deputy hath sent out a warrant to stay the landing of any of these Scotch that came without a certificate.

Belfast, which was to become the largest city in Northern Ireland, was granted to Sir Arthur Chichester, a Devon man, in 1604. He received a grant of this territory and in 1613 the tiny settlement received a charter of incorporation with the right of returning two members to Parliament. Sir Arthur Chichester was appointed Lord Deputy in 1604 and in 1612 he was created

Baron Chichester of Belfast. During this period many of his supporters secured estates to the south of Belfast, particularly in the Malone area, ensuring that north Down was noticeably English in character. The commissioners sent to report on the progress of the Plantation in 1611 found:

> The Towne of Bealfast is plotted out in good forme, wherein are many famelyes of English Scottish and some Manksmen already inhabitinge of which some are artificers who have buylte good tymber houses with chimneyes after the fashion of the English palle and one Inn with very good lodginges which is a great comforte to the Travellers in those partes.

In 1641 a number of Irish chieftains who had earlier been dispossessed of their land, or feared that such a fate was about to befall them, attempted to drive the settlers from Ulster and plunged the country into more than ten years of bloody fighting. In the summer of 1649 Oliver Cromwell arrived in Ireland accompanied by an army with the object of regaining control of Ireland and avenging the colonists who were massacred in 1641. This he did with characteristic ruthlessness. Those lands belonging to Irish insurgents were confiscated and split up for division between adventurers and soldiers under the supervision of a commission of the revenue established at Carrickfergus headed by the governor, Colonel Arthur Hill of Hillsborough. Most soldiers sold their land cheaply to their officers and returned to their homes. At the same time many Catholic tenantry drifted back to the confiscated territories. Nevertheless, Catholic landowners had been replaced by army officers and those Protestant landowners already established since the Plantation. They were reinforced by a new wave of immigrants from Scotland towards the end of the century driven across the Irish Sea by a series of bad harvests and famine.

Belfast recovered from the wars of the seventeenth century but its progress was unremarkable until the middle of the eighteenth century. It surprised visitors to the town that for much of its formative history Belfast remained in the hands of a single family, the descendants of Arthur Chichester, later 1st Earl of Donegall. They remained absentee landlords for much of the eighteenth century and the town fell into a steady decline precipitated by short leases. Lord Massereene, who in 1752 was resident in the town, complained that it was 'in a ruinous condition, and will lose both its Trade and Inhabitants if it is not speedily supported by proper tenures'. It was the 5th Earl, who inherited the title in 1757, who at last granted the long leases that enabled Belfast to emerge as the principal town in the North of Ireland by the end of the century.

New buildings and new streets emerged and a stagecoach to Dublin which could do the journey in about a day improved communications with the capital. Edward Willes, Chief Baron of the Irish Exchequer, visited Belfast in 1759 while on circuit in Ireland. He thought it 'a larger town than Warwick and a place of great trade'. He summarised the busy town for the Earl of Warwick:

It is a sea port and through the middle of this town is a canal like Fleet ditch by means of which ships of burthen come up into the middle of the town. Every house in this town belongs to Lord Donegall and a great part of the lands between this and Carrickfergus which is eight miles further. The leases will all be out in a very few years and then it will make his estate immense. The bridge over which we pass into the town is the longest in His Majesty's dominions. It is built over an arm of the sea and a lough, which is great part of it dry at low water: they say it is a mile long, but it is I really believe three quarters of an English mile. This bridge is the mall where all the company of Belfast take the air in a summer's evening.

Belfast was by that time well on its way to becoming the industrial power-house of the North of Ireland. In 1777 the town's first cotton mill was built in Francis Street paving the way for Belfast to become the centre of Ireland's cotton industry. At the turn of the century one visitor found that a good cotton weaver could earn 'from eighteen shillings to a guinea per week, more than double the wages of a linen weaver . . . and a smart young cotton weaver became no slight attraction in the eyes of a cotton belle'. It is estimated that by the end of the eighteenth century, within a radius of 15 miles from Belfast, there were as many as 8,000 people regularly employed in the cotton trade.

Belfast Lough, The Scenery and Antiquities of Ireland, *drawn by* W H Bartlett (1841).

During the eighteenth century Belfast also became a major centre of the linen industry. At first the town was the commercial heart of the industry rather than a manufac-turing centre. Merchants imported potash and oil of vitriol for bleaching and they soon acquired the bulk of the linen export trade. By the 1770s more than a fifth of the linen exported from Ireland was shipped from Belfast. The construction of the

White Linen Hall in 1784, where drapers could market their finished cloth, was an indication of the importance of the linen trade to the growing town. According to the *Belfast News-Letter* of 28 June 1785:

> From the very large and complete assortment of linens at this market, and the attendance of so many of the principal English and Scottish buyers, we understand that both buyers and sellers agree in declaring that they now look upon our White Linen Market as certainly established . . . Our quays at present and during the last week furnished a very agreeable spectacle; the ships for London, Chester, Liverpool, Whitehaven, Workington and Glasgow ranged in a line and gaily dressed with colours and streamers flying, taking in their cargoes of white linens sold in our Hall.

During the first thirty years of the nineteenth century the cotton and linen industries helped transform Belfast from a small town into a major industrial city. By the 1820s there were 20 cotton mills employing 3,500 people in Belfast. Already the cotton industry was being eclipsed by the newly mechanised linen mills. In 1828, Mulholland's York Street cotton factory burned down. It was replaced by a 5-storey factory with 3 steam engines driving some 8,000 flax spinning spindles. The new operation was such a success that other cotton spinners began to adapt their mills for spinning flax. In 1830 there were 2 linen mills, by 1850 there were 32 with over ½ million spindles and Belfast was well on its way to replacing Leeds and Dundee as the major linen manufacturer in the country. William Makepeace Thackeray, soon to become famous as the author of *Vanity Fair*, visited Belfast during the early 1840s:

> They call Belfast the Irish Liverpool; if people are for calling names, it would be better to call it the Irish London at once – the chief city of the kingdom, at any rate. It looks hearty, thriving, and prosperous, as if it had money in its pockets, and roast-beef for dinner: it has no pretensions to fashion, but looks, mayhap better in its honest broadcloth than *some people* in their shabby brocade. The houses are as handsome as at Dublin, with this advantage, that the people seem to live in them. They have no attempt at ornament, for the most part, but are grave, stout. Red-brick edifices, laid out at four angles in orderly streets and squares.

During the second half of the nineteenth century Belfast grew more rapidly than any other city in the British Isles. Its prosperity largely founded on the textile industry was further enhanced by the development of the shipbuilding and engineering firms which became major employers in the town. The growth of these industries heralded an immense influx of workmen from the surrounded countryside, especially Antrim and Down. But many were attracted to Belfast from Tyrone, Londonderry, Donegal and Armagh by the promise of high wages. During the second half of the nineteenth century the population of Belfast rose from 90,000 to 350,000. Only by constantly redrawing the city's boundary could Dublin keep its coveted position as the largest city in Ireland. In 1888 Queen Victoria granted Belfast city status, and four years later another charter conferred on the Mayor the title of 'Lord Mayor'. This charter declared that Belfast was the capital of the Province of Ulster and that in commercial and manufacturing it was the first town in Ireland. The extension of the city boundary was authorised by the Belfast Corporation Act of 1896 and now included Greencastle on the north, Shaw's Bridge on the south, Knock on the east and Wolfhill House on the west.

The great industrialists and businessmen of Belfast looked to Britain and the Empire for markets and raw materials. They had more in common with their counterparts on Merseyside and Clydeside than they did with the rest of Ireland. They reacted with alarm to the issue of Irish Home Rule, which dominated British political affairs from the 1870s until the end of the First World War. Both supporters and opponents of Home Rule put various interpretations on the term, and it took a British Prime Minister, William Ewart Gladstone, to give it concrete form by offering an Irish parliament responsibility for purely domestic affairs. By the twentieth century, Belfast was firmly established as the centre of Unionist resistance to Home Rule. Ulster Unionists were convinced that Home Rule would, in the words of the Solemn League and Covenant, 'be disastrous to the material well-being of Ulster as well as the whole of Ireland, subversive of our civil and religious freedom, destructive of our citizenship, and perilous to the unity of the Empire' and on 28 September 1912 ¼ million of them pledged themselves to 'resist using all means which may be found necessary to defeat the present conspiracy to set up a Home Rule Parliament in Ireland'.

The Third Home Rule Bill of 1912 resulted in the formation of the Ulster Volunteer Force in January 1913. With a membership estimated at 90,000, the UVF were backed by the Conservative Party in Westminster and its leader Andrew Bonar Law, himself of Ulster decent. The situation was made even more impossible for the government on the 26 July when the Irish Volunteers, now some 160,000 strong, landed around 1,500 rifles and 45,000 rounds of ammunition at Howth harbour outside Dublin. Only the outbreak of the First World War prevented the drift towards civil war in

Ireland. By the end of the war Ulster Unionists had revived the UVF and secured the exclusion of the six counties of north-east Ulster from a Dublin parliament when Ireland was partitioned in 1921. Instead, a parliament was established in Belfast which was initially boycotted by Nationalists. From the moment of its inception the Northern Ireland government was faced with communal violence and economic uncertainty. As community relations deteriorated throughout the 1920s and 1930s the staple industries of linen and shipbuilding went into steep decline. The Second World War created further divisions as the Irish Free State remained neutral. Northern Ireland strategic importance to the Allied cause was acknowledged by Winston Churchill at the end of the war:

> That was a dark and dangerous hour. We were alone, and had to fight single-handed the full fury of the German attack raining down death and destruction on our cities and, still more deadly, seeking to strangle our life by cutting off the entry to our ports of the ships which brought us our food and the weapons we so sorely needed. Only one great channel of entry remained open. That channel remained open because loyal Ulster gave us the full use of the Northern Irish ports and waters, and thus ensured the free working of the Clyde and the Mersey. But for the loyalty of Northern Ireland and its devotion to what had now become the cause of thirty Governments or Nations we should have been confronted with slavery and death, and the light which now shines so strongly throughout the world would have been quenched.

By the late 1960s violence had returned to the streets of Belfast and British troops were called in as a short-term measure to restore order. They were still there more than thirty years later. In 1972 direct rule was imposed by Westminster but by that time Belfast and many towns in Northern Ireland were witnessing terrorist warfare on an unprecedented scale. It would be a quarter of a century before a parliament would once again meet in Belfast. The new Northern Ireland Assembly has now brought a considerable measure of stability to Northern Ireland, and one of the chief dividends of the new political process has been a dramatic increase in visitors to the Province from all over the world.

Today a quarter of the population of Northern Ireland lives in Belfast. The city has been revitalised in recent years with major shopping developments, hotels and restaurants breathing new life into the city centre. Those who visit Northern Ireland today in search of their ancestors can still see evidence of Northern Ireland's Victorian past, particularly in Belfast when it was one of the major cities of the British Empire. No part of the city is more than a few minutes walk from the surrounding countryside and most streets offer a view of rolling hills or mountains. As a recent guide book puts it: 'Belfast is quite unlike any other city, Irish or British. Its unique charisma derives from a curious mixture of identities, its sense of separateness, and, of course, the notoriety it has received as a centre of conflict. Belfast combines the hard-headed proletarian quality of a large industrial town with the dignified self-confidence of a respectable and well-to-do provincial capital.'

Chapter 1

WHERE TO BEGIN

Once bitten by the need to trace your family tree it is very tempting to rush to the nearest archival institution and to be put off immediately by the daunting amount of information available. It is therefore best to begin your research at home. Start with yourself, work through your parents to your grandparents and take each generation as you find it. Searching through old records, although often rewarding, is apt to be perplexing and frustrating. Even the most experienced researcher can take a wrong turn and end up spending valuable time ploughing through records that only lead to a dead end. To make more productive use of your time, it is essential to gather as much information as possible from old family Bibles, legal documents (such as wills or leases) and inscriptions from family gravestones. This can help to pinpoint exactly where your family lived at a particular time and provide vital clues to add to names that family historians are often disappointed to find are all too popular in Northern Ireland.

It is also essential to talk to relatives, especially those from an older generation whose memories, however inaccurate, may point you in the right direction. Conversations or correspondence can lead you to other, more distant relatives or friends of the family, of whose existence you were previously unaware. If you are lucky you may find someone who has taken an interest in the family history, perhaps has even made a start at a family tree. They may be able to tell you if there were certain occupations or trades associated with the family, or which schools and churches they attended, perhaps where they were buried. You may find out that the family are associated with a particular town or townland, and that a particular first name has been passed down through the generations. Ask them if anyone has served in the armed forces or if relatives have emigrated. If you are very fortunate they may have in their possession old letters, diaries, wills or birth certificates that will save you time and money.

What do I need to know?

To make best use of the records it is essential to know where your ancestors lived in Northern Ireland. Linking your ancestor to a county is a great help, but what your really need to do is to identify the parish or townland of origin. The county based heritage centres in Northern Ireland can help. Established as part of the Irish Genealogical Project, which aims to create a comprehensive genealogical database for the entire island of Ireland, each centre indexes and computerises records of a particular county, or in some cases two counties. Staff will search their databases for a fee. If you only know the name of the county your ancestor came from, one of these centres may be the best way of finding a more specific place of origin.

A walk round a graveyard

If you know where your ancestor lived it is worth paying a visit to the local graveyard as a headstone may provide important information, such as names and dates of births and deaths, and this will make it easier to search through old records. Other valuable information can include the deceased's occupation or place of origin and even include the names of husbands, wives or children. They may reveal the married names of daughters or sisters of your ancestors and may record two, three or more generations of a family. The style of the headstone can also give a clue to the economic circumstances of the family at a particular period in history. You should, however, treat the information on a headstone (especially ages) with some care. A memorial may refer to two or more people and it may have been placed there on the death of the last person, perhaps many years after the death of the first person buried in the plot.

Because so many headstones can be illegible it is worth checking at your local library to find out if the gravestones in a particular cemetery have been transcribed and published. Most Northern Ireland graveyards are also listed at: www.historyfromheadstones.com.

Surnames

It is widely believed that there are only two kinds of surname in Northern Ireland. Those surnames that owe their origins to native Gaelic families and those brought to Northern Ireland by more recent settlers from England and Scotland. In fact, when compared with Wales, Ireland has a wide variety of surnames which reveal a much more complex picture of Irish society than simply native versus newcomer.

A scene from a contemporary woodcut detailing the Nine Years War, by John Derricke, British Library.

Ireland was one of the first countries to evolve a system of hereditary surnames. They emerged during the eleventh century as the population increased. For centuries the social circle of most people was small and families lived their lives side-by-side with the same families for generation after generation. As the population grew and more than one person with the same name lived locally it became necessary to have a more precise identification. At first the surname was formed by prefixing Mc (meaning son of) to the father's Christian name or O (meaning grandson) to that of a grandfather or earlier ancestor. Many people believe that the Mc is a sign of Scottish origin. However, names like McMahon, McGuire, McNamara, McCarthy, etc. are essentially Irish names.

Later names were formed by the occupation of the father, as, for example, Mc an Bhaird, son of the bard (modern McWard and Ward), or O hIceadha-icidhe, doctor or healer (modern Hickey). Sometimes the name denoted a particular feature or peculiarity of the grandfather or father such as Mc Dubhghaill, black stranger (modern McDowell). Sometimes a nickname was incorporated such as Mc an Mhadaidh-mada, meaning dog (now McAvaddy).

It is important to note that there may be wide variations in the spelling of surnames. The introduction of the English language and the fact that legal and official documents were often prepared by clerks who had no knowledge of the Irish language contributed to this. Names were often anglicised to a form in English that was close to the sound of the Gaelic. Therefore O Dubhthaigh became O'Duffy and then Duffy. Also rare names were often absorbed by better known ones of somewhat similar sound, for example, Sullahan changed to Sullivan. The name Cullen is a good example of this. It is among the 100 most common in Ireland and is mainly found in Leinster, where it is an anglicisation of O Cuilinn (holly).

However, the name is also found in Scotland, either from the burgh of Cullen in Banffshire, or the Ayrshire and Galloway name which probably has Irish origins.

Throughout Northern Ireland many surnames have become associated with a particular geographical location. McGuiness and McCartan are, for example, most closely associated with County Down, while Maguire is found chiefly in Fermanagh and McDonald in Antrim. The proximity of the English and Scottish coasts also ensured that many names in County Down owed their origins to settlers who arrived long before the Plantation of Ulster. During the twelfth century the Normans established forts at Newry, Downpatrick and Dromore and the colony that they founded extended along the south-eastern coast of County Down. During the centuries that followed the Anglo-Norman colonists were absorbed into the native Gaelic population. However, their names, including Hackett, Jordan, Logan, Whites, Russell and Savage, remain associated with that part of County Down.

In England surnames developed around the twelfth and thirteenth centuries. They were based on a first name, such as Johnson; on a place or locality, such as Hill or Park; on a nickname, such as Redhead or Trench (meaning sleek); or occupation, such as Cooper or Carpenter. Surnames such as Adams, Andrews, Baker, Bingham, Harris, Mitchell, Hunter, Shaw and Turner are just some of the examples that are commonly found in Ulster thanks to the seventeenth-century Plantation.

Less well known is the number of Welsh settlers who came to Northern Ireland. For more than 400 years before the Plantation they migrated to Ireland. Names such as Branagh, Lynnott and Merrick are examples of Welsh settlement in Ireland. The surname Walsh, the third most common in Ireland, like the surname Wallace in Scotland, is derived from the Old English word *woelisc*, meaning 'foreigner' and *le Waleis*, 'the Welshman'.

One should not take it for granted that an English or Scottish surname invariably means that an ancestor was of settler stock. For example, the name Hughes, the second commonest in County Armagh and widespread in Wales and England, is not exclusive to those whose ancestors migrated to Ulster in the seventeenth century. A significant number are in fact from native stock, descendants of the several O hAodha (O'Hugh) septs or of the Mc Aodha (McHugh) septs, whose forebears adopted Hughes as their surname. The same may be said of the surname Campbell, one of the commonest in Scotland. Some who bear this surname may be descended from the native Irish sept based in County Tyrone, Mc Cathmhaoil.

It is ironic that, given Northern Ireland's reputation for religious conflict, settlers from many parts of the world have fled to Ireland because of persecution. The Huguenots, for example, fled their native France settling in many parts of Ireland. They made a major contribution to the development of the linen industry in Ulster and Huguenot surnames such as Alderdice, Latour, Ricard and Duprey are their most enduring legacy.

Those wishing to find out more about the origin and location of surnames should consult the following:

Bell, Robert, *The Book of Ulster Surnames* (Belfast, 1989)
Black, George F, *The Surnames of Scotland: Their Origin, Meaning and History* (New York, 1962)
de Breffny, Brian, *Irish Family Names, Arms, Origins and Locations* (Dublin, 1982)
Grehan, Ida, *Irish Family Names, Highlights of 50 Family Histories* (London, 1973)
MacLysaght, Edward, *Irish Families*, 3rd edn (Dublin, 1972)
MacLysaght, Edward, *More Irish Families* (Dublin, 1960), supplement to *Irish Families* (Dublin, 1957)
MacLysaght, Edward, *The Surnames of Ireland*, 3rd edn (Dublin, 1978)
Matheson, Robert E, *Special Report on Surnames in Ireland* (Dublin, 1894)
Morgan, T J and Prys Morgan, *Welsh Surnames* (Cardiff, 1985)
O'Laughlin, M, *The Master Book of Irish Surnames* (Belfast, 1988)
Quinn, Sean E, *Surnames in Ireland* (Bray, 2000)
Reaney, P H, *A Dictionary of British Surnames* (London, 1958)

Also of interest is *Grenham's Irish Surnames*, by John Grenham, produced in 2002. This CD-ROM provides an unparalleled resource for anyone interested in Irish surnames. It includes details of 26,756 Irish surnames and 104,058 surname variants, an extensive bibliography of Irish family history, Ireland-wide parish maps and details of the records of 3,782 churches and congregations throughout Ireland, comprising 8,376 sets of records. In addition, the CD-ROM includes a fully context-sensitive Windows Help file detailing the sources used and providing detailed help at all times, and a user-friendly interface designed to make the search process as easy as possible.

Visiting the archives

The Public Record Office of Northern Ireland (PRONI)

PRONI was established under the Public Records Act (Northern Ireland) 1923, and opened in March 1924 in Belfast. What makes PRONI different from other archival institutions in the British Isles is the unique combination of private and official records. PRONI is at once Public Record Office, manuscripts department of a national library and county record office for the six counties of Northern Ireland. This range of remit ensured that PRONI was to be a repository for court and departmental records and also a place of deposit for privately owned archives. It is of incalculable benefit to students, genealogists and members of the public that archival material of whatever provenance from within Northern Ireland, and in some cases from outside Northern Ireland, is all gathered together, preserved and made available in one place.

Records fall into three major categories: records of government departments, some going back to the early nineteenth century; records of courts of law, local authorities and non-departmental public bodies; and records deposited by private individuals, estates, churches, businesses and institutions. PRONI also holds copies of the 1901 census for the six counties of Northern Ireland, which are available in the self-service Microfilm Room.

PRONI's eCatalogue, containing over 1 million catalogue entries, is now available online for searching and browsing. The eCatalogue contains approximately 60 per cent of PRONI's total catalogue entries, with the remainder to be published on an ongoing basis. Visit the PRONI website for more details at: www.proni.gov.uk/index.htm.

The Linen Hall Library

The Linen Hall Library was founded in 1788 as the Belfast Reading Society and is the oldest library in Belfast. It is also the last-surviving subscribing library in Ireland. The library houses more than 250,000 volumes, 75,000 pamphlets and significant holdings of periodicals, newspapers, manuscripts, maps, microforms, photographs, films and recordings. It maintains a general lending and reference collection, the latter being especially strong in genealogy, heraldry, history and travel. Its great strength, however, is its Irish and local-studies collection, with particular focus on Belfast and Counties Antrim and Down. The 'Genealogical Collection' includes some 5,000 volumes, mainly of Ulster interest and Scottish and American connections, plus Army, Church and educational lists.

The Central Library

The Central Library, opened in 1888, is a major research and reference library. It is part of the Belfast Education and Library Board, which operates another twenty branch libraries throughout the city. The collection includes in the region of a million volumes, plus the largest newspaper collection in Northern Ireland. The library has a newspaper cuttings index covering the eighteenth and nineteenth centuries which may provide a short cut to finding information in the papers. The library does not offer genealogical services per se, but its holdings in this area are extensive, and staff are willing to assist researchers as far as possible.

Local libraries

Each county and most major towns in Northern Ireland have a main library. Many of these libraries have a local and family history collection. These collections may include estate records, newspapers, gravestone inscriptions, minute books of various local and county government agencies, Poor Law records, family pedigrees and histories. Some libraries have indexed parts of their collections. County or specialty museums may also contain genealogical records, including estate, military, tax, Church and business or employment records. For addresses of Irish libraries and museums, see Seamus Helferty and Raymond Refausse, eds, *Directory of Irish Archives*.

Family history centres

From 1948 the Mormon Church began microfilming documentary material in Ireland and their holdings include some baptismal and marriage registers for Roman Catholic parishes and some other denominations. The most important resources acquired at that time were the registers of births, deaths and marriages as well as the indexes to these records held in the Registrar General's Office, Custom House, Dublin. The Mormon Church has indexed most of the 2 million reels of microfilm that they hold and these indexes are made available on an International Genealogical Index (IGI). This index is arranged both by county and surname and is available in many libraries and record offices and also on the Internet. Access to the IGI is free of charge, as is the viewing of films held in the Mormon Family History Centres at Londonderry, Coleraine and Belfast.

Heritage or genealogical centres

Local heritage centres, sometimes called genealogical centres, are a recent development in Ireland and are run on a commercial basis. The majority of these centres are currently indexing Church records, mainly Roman Catholic parish registers. Some centres are also indexing tithe applotment books, Griffith's *Primary Valuation*, the 1901 census and gravestone inscriptions. The centres are in the process of computerising their indexes.

Centre records are not open to the public. Centre staff, however, will search their indexes (they hold no original records, only indexes!) and supply information for a fee. A list of those covering Northern Ireland is available in the Appendix.

Societies

The North of Ireland Family History Society celebrated its twenty-fifth anniversary in 2008. Beginning with a family history group in Bangor it has mushroomed into ten other branches and hundreds of members worldwide. Its objective is to foster interest in family history with special reference to families who have roots in the Northern of Ireland and their descendants. This is done by means of monthly meetings with specialist speakers, research evenings and visits to local archives. The society is not a research agency, but members are happy to put people in contact with one another.

DNA

Less than twenty years ago, DNA was a term most people encountered only in science textbooks. Now it is part of our everyday lives and vocabulary, thanks partly to the media obsession with cloning and to the popularity of shows like CSI where DNA is a vital element of the detective work.

DNA is now also becoming more significant in genealogical research. Many Irish clans have DNA surname projects with the objective of identification of a place of origin of the family, completing a more precise history of the clan and providing a link between those of the surname who have emigrated and where there is a gap in the records. By taking a test you are primarily seeking to identify someone who shares your surname whose DNA results are identical (or nearly identical) to your own. If you find this kind of match the two of you could be related to each other within a genealogical timeframe. You should then compare family trees in a bid to find the male ancestor through whom you are mutually linked.

The value of such projects is particularly obvious for those with Irish ancestors who do not know their place of origin in Ireland. An exact or almost-exact match with someone in Ireland who knows their place of origin can provide a vital clue to their ancestral homeland. For a list of those clans involved in DNA projects see www.theclansofireland.ie-/dna.htm.

A number of firms exist to help those who wish to have their DNA tested. These include:

www.familygenetics.co.uk/
www.dnaheritage.com/
www.oxfordancestors.co.uk/
www.familytreedna.com.

For more information see Megan Smolenyak Smolenyak and Ann Turner, *Trace Your Roots with DNA* (Rodale, 2004).

Chapter 2

CENSUS RECORDS

Once the researcher has located the area in which his or her ancestors lived it is then a matter of pinpointing the records that have survived for that particular area. At first glance, Irish census returns would seem to be an obvious place for family historians to begin their search. The census is basically a head count of every person living in Northern Ireland from the youngest children to the oldest inhabitant of the household. It was therefore an immeasurable disaster when the census records before 1861 were destroyed during the Irish Civil War in 1922 and those from 1861–91 were pulped into waste paper during the First World War. However, returns for a small number of parishes have survived.

1821

This census was organised by townland, civil parish, barony and county and took place on 28 May 1821. Almost all the original returns were destroyed in 1922, with only a few volumes surviving for Counties Fermanagh and Armagh, PRONI reference MIC/5A and MIC/15A. A copy of the 1821 Forkhill parish census, which lists 6,344 individuals, was recently unearthed by a researcher. Armagh Ancestry has now computerised these census returns, which can be accessed for a fee online at: brsgenealogy.com/armagh/logi...t_url=quis.php.

1831

Once again, this census was organised by townland, civil parish, barony and county. It also includes the name, age, occupation and religion of the occupants. Very little of this census survives, with most of the remaining fragments relating to County Londonderry:
MIC/5A/6 Barony of Coleraine;

Raphael Street, Belfast, 1912, Welch Collection, Ulster Museum.

MIC/5A/6 Barony of Coleraine;

MIC/5A/6 to 7 City of Londonderry;

MIC/5A/8 Barony of Loughlinsholin;

MIC/5A/9 Barony of Tirkeeran.

1841

Unfortunately, no part of the census for Northern Ireland has survived.

1851

Taken on 30 March 1851, this government census added a column for religious affiliation. Most of the surviving returns relate to County Antrim: MIC/5A/11–26. There are also individual census returns for various parts of the Province in MIC/15A.

1861, 1871, 1881 and 1891

The census records for 1861 to 1891 were destroyed by order of the government during the First World War. Nothing survives for the Northern Ireland area.

1901

On 31 March 1901, a census was taken of the whole island of Ireland. The original returns are deposited at the National Archives; microfilm copies of the returns for Northern Ireland are available at PRONI. The census records:

- Names;

- Relationship to the head of the household;

- Religion;

- Literacy;

- Occupation;

- Age;

- Marital status;

- County of birth;

- Ability to speak English or Irish.

Every town, village and townland for Ireland is represented and those inhabitants who were at home on 31 March 1901 are listed.

The original census returns for Northern Ireland are held by the National Archives in Dublin. A catalogue is available on the open shelves in the Reading Room. Each country is listed in a separate volume. The records are numerically arranged by District Electoral Division (DED) and held in bound volumes. Before consulting the 1901 census returns, you must establish in which DED the relevant townland or street is situated. The DED was based on the subdivision of the old Poor Law Union and was used for electoral purposes. The DED, with a number attached, can be found in the 1901 *Townland Index*, which is available on the shelves of the Search Room. Simply look up the relevant townland, village or town and you will find it listed along with the barony and Poor Law Union.

Within each DED the townlands are arranged alphabetically and numerically. In order to request the returns for a particular townland you must include the name of the country, the number of the DED and the number of the townland. The returns for 1901 are bound into large volumes.

The 1901 census is available on microfilm at PRONI under reference MIC/354. Once again it is necessary to find out the relevant DED. This can be done by consulting the 1901 *Townland Index*, which is available on the shelves of the Public Search Room. Each DED is listed in a series of calendars which will give you the appropriate reel number.

1911

The 1911 census was taken on 1 April of that year and, while including the same information as the 1901 census, also contains additional facts such as the number of years a wife was married, the number of children born and the number still living. This census is not yet available at PRONI because of the more restrictive UK 'hundred-year closure rule' on access, but microfilms of the original census returns can be viewed at the NAI.

In order to locate the relevant DED number, the townland, town or street number it is necessary to consult the 1911 Census Catalogue, available on the open shelves. Sometimes this number corresponds with the number used in 1901, but in many cases it does not. The number used in 1911 is usually close to the 1901 number. If the 1911 DED number cannot be found, help should be sought from the Search Room staff in the NAI.

It is important to realise that there were boundary changes in townlands and DEDs between 1901 and 1911; an official Parliamentary Paper listing these changes was published. Unlike the 1901 census returns, which are held in large bound volumes, those for 1911 are unbound and stored in folders within boxes. Both censuses are arranged by Poor Law Union, DED, county, barony, parish, townland and street, if in a town or city.

1901 and 1911 censuses online

The Irish Census Project is currently digitising over 3,000 census microfilm reels, and creating 2 indexes linked to the digital images: a topographical index based on townland/street within DEDs, and a nominal index to every individual listed in both censuses. So far only 1911 has been digitised. Census returns for Antrim, Armagh, Down, Fermanagh and Tyrone are available online at: www.census.nationalarchives.ie.

Old-age pension claims

The old-age pension search forms held by PRONI are an under-used source by genealogists. They are of great interest because they contain extracts from the 1841 and 1851 censuses, which were almost completely destroyed. The old-age pension was introduced on 1 January 1909 for those over 70 years of age. For many born before 1864, when the state registration of births began in Ireland, it was necessary to pay for a search to be made of the 1841 and 1851 censuses in order to prove their entitlement to the pension. The 'form 37s', which were submitted by local pensions offices, include the applicant's name, stated age, parents' names and address at the time of the census. Details of the search were added to the form, and each claim was bound according to barony in a series of volumes relating to claimants. Those for Northern Ireland are held at PRONI (T/550/2–37). There are also some individual returns in MIC/15A.

A partial index is available on microfiche (reference MF/9/1/1–9), but its entries relate to the Mormon microfilm copy and do not always correspond to the originals.

The following extract is taken from Form 37s for County Fermanagh held by PRONI, reference T/550/21.

Census year for which search is requested

1851
Claimant: Bernard McCabe
Claimant's Father: John McCabe
Claimant's Mother: Isabelle

John McCabe	46	Head
Isabelle	35	Wife
Catherine	14	Daughter
Mary	12	"
Isabelle	9	"
Bridget	5	"
James	3	Son
No death or absentee		
Townland: Doagh Clebe	Parish: Devenish	Barony: Magheraboy

Chapter 3

CIVIL REGISTRATION

C ivil or state registration of all births, deaths and marriages began in Ireland on 1 January 1864. This was nearly thirty years later than similar legislation was passed in England and Wales, and ten years after Scotland. Provisions had been made from 1 April 1845 to enable the registration of non-Catholic marriages in Ireland and for the appointment of registrars, who were also given the power to solemnise marriages by civil contract. These provisions, based on the legislation introduced in England and Wales, empowered the Established Church to register the marriages, but marriages in other churches were to be registered by a civil registrar. In Ireland the Roman Catholic Church was concerned that this latter requirement might detract from the religious nature of the marriage ceremony and they were consequently excluded from the legislation.

Pressure for the compulsory recording of births, deaths and marriages in Ireland reached its peak in the mid-Victorian period. Members of the Presbyterian community complained that the absence of this facility made it very difficult to establish rights of inheritance and noted that those of its members seeking commissions in the Indian service could not show proof of their age or origins. The Irish Poor Law Commissioners were also finding it very difficult to impose compulsory vaccination against smallpox because of the absence of information about births and deaths. Eventually, in 1863, a bill providing for the registration of births and deaths in Ireland was introduced and passed. While the Act did not encompass Catholic marriages, a Private Members' Bill was successfully introduced later that year which resulted in the civil registration by the state of marriages celebrated according to the rites of the Catholic Church, ensuring a complete Irish civil registration system was at last in place.

Although registrars were responsible for the actual registers themselves and for their safe-keeping, the legal obligation to register births, deaths and marriages rested with the public. This legal obligation was backed by

North Gate, Carrickfergus, The Story of Belfast *by Mary Lowry, c. 1913.*

heavy fines for failure to register. Nevertheless, although there was a fine of £1 for the wilful neglect to register a birth, frequent examples of applicants for old-age pensions in the 1930s and 1940s who found it difficult to establish their claim suggests that many births were not recorded in the 1860s and 1870s.

Birth certificates

The first significant evidence of an individual's life is, since 1864, his or her birth certificate. From this we can learn where a person was born, the names of the parents, the maiden name of the mother, and the occupation of the father. This gives the researcher many important clues with which to move back to a previous generation.

Birth certificates normally give the name of the child, but in some cases only the sex is recorded, i.e., the child had not been given a name by the time the birth was registered. The name and residence of the father is registered. Although this is usually the same as the place of birth of the child, in some cases it will show that the father was working abroad or in another part of Ireland when the child was born. The mother's maiden name is provided as well as her first name. Finally, the name and address of the informant is recorded, together with his or her qualification to sign. This will usually be the father or mother or someone present at the birth, such as a midwife or even the child's grandmother.

It is important to treat the dates on Irish birth certificates with a degree of caution. As a general rule, the younger the child was when registered, the more accurate the birth date written in the official register. The longer families waited to register the child the more chance that the date given is inaccurate. Families were also prepared to change the date of birth if the child was more than three months old to avoid paying the late-registration penalty.

Marriage certificates

Civil records of marriage normally given fuller information than birth and death certificates, and are the most useful of civil records. Information on the individuals getting married includes their name, age status, and occupation. The names and occupations of their fathers are also given. The church, the officiating minister and the witnesses to the ceremony are named. In most cases the exact age of the parties is not registered, and the entry will simply read 'full age' (i.e., over 21) or 'minor' (i.e., under 21). If the father of one of the parties was no longer living this may be indicated in the marriage certificate, but in many cases it is not. The fact that marriage certificates had to be filed within three days of the marriage ceremony means that marriage dates are generally accurate.

Death certificates

Civil records of death in Ireland are sadly rather uninformative. The name of the deceased is given together with the date, place and cause of death, marital status, the age of death and occupation. The name and address of the informant is also recorded. Usually this is the person present at the time of the death who may be a close family member, or even an employee or servant.

The indexes

Indexes to civil marriages 1845–63 are handwritten, but thereafter all indexes are printed. From 1864 to 1877 indexes for births, marriages and deaths consist of a single yearly volume covering the whole of Ireland. From 1878 the annual indexes were arranged on a quarterly basis. In each index the surnames will be arranged alphabetically, followed by the first names. The name of the superintendent registrar's district is also given, followed by the volume number and page number of the master copies of the registers in Dublin.

General Register Office, Belfast, and district registrars' offices

The General Register Office (GRO) in Belfast holds the original birth and death registers recorded by the local district registrars for Northern Ireland from 1864. Marriage registers are available from 1922. The following computerised indexes to the civil registers are available:

- Birth indexes – 1864 onwards;
- Death indexes – 1864 onwards;
- Marriage indexes – 1845 onwards.

If you wish to search the indexes yourself (only indexes are available for public inspection, not the registers themselves), it is possible to visit the GRO, if you have arranged a time and date in advance. An index search costs £10 for a period not exceeding 6 hours. This includes four verifications of items found in the indexes, with the option of further verifications of items found in the indexes at £2.50 each. An assisted search service is also provided. This can be a much quicker method of extracting information from the civil registers, especially if a specific location is known, but costs £19 per hour. A full certified copy of a birth, death or marriage certificate costs £11.

The GRO also holds records of a more specialised nature. These include:

- Records of still births occurring in Northern Ireland on or after 1 January 1961. These registers are not open for public search;

- Records of persons adopted under orders made by courts in Northern Ireland on or after 1 January 1931;

- Records of births at sea of children, who were registered on or after 1 January 1922 and one of whose parents was born in Northern Ireland;

- Records of deaths at sea of persons born in Northern Ireland where death was registered on or after 1 January 1922;

- Records of births of children whose father was born in Northern Ireland, deaths and marriages registered on or after 1 January 1927 by way of the Army Act 1879;

- Records of births of children of Northern Ireland parents born abroad and registered by British Consuls on or after 1 January 1922;

- Records of deaths of Northern Ireland persons registered by British Consuls abroad on or after 1 January 1922;

- Records of marriages of Northern Ireland persons registered by British Consuls on and after 1 January 1923;

- Records of births, deaths and marriages of Northern Ireland persons registered by the British High Commissioner in Commonwealth countries on or after 1 January 1950;

- Certified copies of certificates (with translations) relating to marriages of persons from Northern Ireland in certain foreign countries according to the laws of these countries, without the presence of a British Consular Officer;

• Records of deaths of persons born in Northern Ireland who died on war service between 1939 and 1948.

The GRO is located at Oxford House, 49–55 Chichester Street, Belfast BT1 4HL. Applications for certificates can be made in person, by post, by telephone (028 9025 2000) or online, at: www.groni.gov.uk. Searches will be made in the year quoted plus the two years either side unless a wider search is requested. A further fee will be required for each extra five years searched. Personal applications are processed within three working days; postal or telephone applications are processed within eight working days.

Although indexes to civil marriages registers for Northern Ireland are available at the GRO from 1845, the original registers are located at the district registrars' offices at local councils. Applications for marriage certificates can be made directly to them or through the GRO in Belfast.

Church of Latter-Day Saints

From 1948 the Church of the Latter-Day Saints (LDS), or Mormons, began microfilming documentary material in Ireland. The most important resource acquired at that time was the registers of births, deaths and marriages as well as the indexes to these records held in the Registrar General's Office, Custom House, Dublin. Unfortunately, the Mormons

Tully Castle, Illustrated Dublin Journal, *No. 7, 19 October 1861.*

were not able to complete the filming of all registers before work was suspended.

The LDS collection of microfilms of civil registers and indexes is as follows:

- Birth indexes 1864–1959;

- Birth registers 1864 to first quarter 1880; 1900–13;

- Marriage indexes 1845–1959;

- Marriage registers 1845–70;

- Death indexes 1864–1959;

- Death registers 1864–70.

It is important to note that, although there are gaps in the birth registers, microfilm copies of the actual official registers are available to researchers. This is a vital resource, because in the General Register Offices in Dublin, Belfast and London the public have no right of access to the original records. In addition, some parts of the early years of birth registrations appear to be included in the LDS International Genealogical Index, which is searchable online at: www.familysearch.org/, and the 2002 edition of the LDS CD set, *British Isles Vital Records*, which includes an index to birth registrations from 1864 to 1875.

Access to microfilmed copies of the indexes and registers is also free of charge at any of the Mormon Family History Centres. The Family History Library Catalogue is the best way of finding collections in the Family History Library. It is usual to search by place to find the available records for where your ancestors lived. The records are listed by country, county or civil parish, depending on the nature of the records. Within each locality, the records are organised by topic – in this case 'civil registration'.

An excellent introduction and guide to civil registration in Ireland is Catherine Blumsom's *Civil Registration of Births, Deaths and Marriages in Ireland: a Practical Approach*, published by the Ulster Historical Foundation.

Chapter 4

EIGHTEENTH-CENTURY RECORDS

Survey of Downpatrick, 1708

In 1708 James Maguire made a survey of the town of Downpatrick, County Down. He described each premise by name, giving its size, its principal tenant and the half-yearly rent due. A manuscript copy of this survey, made by the Revd David Stewart in 1927, is available at PRONI, D/1759/2A/8 and at the National Library, 94115 p1. A printed copy can be found in *The City of Downe*, Belfast, 1927, by Edward Parkinson.

Protestant Householders, 1740

What has generally been termed a 'census of Protestant householders' was compiled in 1740. The returns were made by the collectors of the hearth money and it has, therefore, been recently suggested that this 'census' is actually a hearth-money roll. It is no more than a list of names arranged by country, barony and parish and, reflecting its supervision by the inspector responsible for collecting hearth money; it is occasionally divided into 'walks'. The original records of this survey were destroyed in Dublin in 1922 but copies survive for part of the survey in transcripts prepared by the genealogist, Tension Groves. Copies are held by PRONI (T/808/15258) and the National Library of Ireland (Ms 4173). A bound transcript copy is available on the open shelves of the Public Search Room at PRONI.

Householders Returns, 1766

In March and April 1766, Church of Ireland rectors were instructed by the Irish House of Lords to 'return a list of the several families in their parishes to this house on the first Monday after the Recess, distinguishing which are Protestants and which are Papists . . .' and giving an account of any Roman Catholic clergy active in their area. No set form was laid down for the provision of this information so the quality of returns varies considerably from parish to parish. Some of the more diligent rectors listed every townland and every household, but many drew up only numerical totals of the population. They generally distinguish between Church of Ireland (Episcopalian), Roman Catholic (termed 'Papists' in the returns) and Presbyterians (or Dissenters) but occasionally details are given for smaller denominations such as Quakers. All of the original returns were destroyed in the Four Courts in 1922, but extensive transcripts survive for the parishes of Seapatrick, Tullynakill, Greyabbey, Inch and Kilbroney. A bound copy can be found on the shelves of the Public Search Room at the Public Record Office of Northern Ireland and a copy is available in the Tension Groves Collection, PRONI reference T/808/15264–7. Copies of the 1766 Householders List can also be found at the Linen Hall Library, Belfast, Armagh Museum, RCB Library, Ms 23; National Library of Ireland Ms 4173; and at Family History Centres, SLC film 1279330. Some originals and transcripts are available at the Genealogical Office, GO 537. A full listing of all surviving manuscripts is available on the shelves of the National Archives Reading Room and online at: www.nationalarchives.ie/genealogy/ReligiousCensus.pdf.

Armagh 'census', 1770

The so-called census of Armagh City includes individual names and occupations. The head of the household is named and it is recorded if they are married. The names of the wives are not recorded, although their religion if different from that of their husband is given. A manuscript edition with an alphabetical index is available at the Robinson Library, Armagh. An indexed typescript copy is also deposited at the Armagh Museum. A number of manuscript copies are deposited at PRONI under the following reference numbers, T/389, T/1228 and T/808/14938, 14977. Copies are also available at the National Library, NL Ms 7370 and at the Family History Centres, SLC film 258621.

The following extract is taken from the 1770 census for Armagh.

English Street

Name	Trade	Children	Servants	Religion
Lord Primates House				
Dr Grueber & w	schoolmaster	–	3 men, 4 maids	EC
Tho McCann & w		8	5	EC
Jn Burgess & w	attorney	3	2 men, 2 maids	EC
Hen Bambrick & w	public house	3		EC
W(ife) Presb				
Graham & w(ife)	cooper			
Wm Hall & w(ife)	public house	2 sons, 2 dau		EC
Alex Murphy & w(ife)	public house			
Jm Greaves & w(ife)	public house	1		EC
Lt Townshend & w(ife)				EC
W(ife) Presb				

Flaxseed Premiums, 1796

As part of a government initiative to encourage the linen trade, free spinning wheels or looms were granted to individuals planting a certain area of land with flax. A ½ acre of flax brought the grower two spinning wheels. A grower of ¼ acre of flax would get one spinning wheel. A flax grower that cultivated no less than 5 acres got a loom or spinning wheels up to the value of 5s. The following quotation is drawn from the conditions set out by the Trustees of the Linen Manufacture.

> To the person who should sow between the 10th day of March and the 1st day of June 1796 with a sufficient quantity of good sound flaxseed, any quantity of land, well prepared and fit for the purpose not less than 1 Acre – 4 Spinning Wheels, 3 Roods – 3 ditto, 2 Roods – 2 ditto and 1 Rood – 1 ditto. And to the person who should sow in like manner any quantity of like land, not less than 5 Acres, a loom or wheels, reels or hatchells to the value of 50 shillings, and for every 5 Acres over and above the first 5, a like premium.

The lists of those entitled to the awards, covering almost 60,000 individuals, were published in 1796. The only copy of the book listing the names of these recipients known to exist until recently was held in the Linen Hall Library, Belfast. Another copy has now been acquired by the Irish Linen Centre in Lisburn Museum. A typescript copy is available on the Search

Room shelves at PRONI, reference T/3419. A surname index for the spinning wheel premium entitlement is also available on microfiche MF7. The Ulster Historical Foundation has computerised this source and it is available on a searchable database on the UHF website. Heritage World had also made it available on CD-ROM.

Catholic migrants from Ulster, 1795–96

Sectarian unrest in the late eighteenth century, particularly in north County Armagh, resulted in many Catholic families leaving Ulster. Many of them ended up in County Mayo. A list of names, and the historical background to these events, can be found in Patrick Tohall, 'The Diamond Fight of 1795 and the resultant expulsions', in *Seanchas Ardmhacha*, vol. 3, no. 1 (1958), 17–50. The information provided includes the name of the individual (or householder) concerned and the parish, and in many cases the townland, from which they originated. The counties covered are Antrim, Armagh, Down, Londonderry, Monaghan and Tyrone. See also 'Petition of Armagh migrants in the Westport', in *Cathair na Mart*, vol. 2, no. 1 (1982).

Records relating to the 1798 rebellion

Antrim and Down were closely associated in the rebellion of 1798. This is

Lurgan volunteer by an unknown artist, Ulster Museum.

hardly surprising given the strongly Presbyterian character of the United Irishmen movement in Ulster. Belfast was an important centre of the movement. In 1791 the Society of United Irishmen was formed in Peggy Barclay's tavern in Crown Entry off High Street. In January 1792 they launched the *Northern Star* to promote the radical cause with Samuel Neilson, owner of Belfast's largest woollen drapery business, as editor. The new organisation spread rapidly to the neighbouring counties of Antrim and Down. Its main aims were parliamentary reform and the removal of English control over Irish affairs.

The rebellion when it came in 1798 was short-lived. It had already collapsed in the south and west of Ireland when the standard was raised in the north. In County Antrim an army of some 3,000 and 4,000 men under Henry Joy McCracken was crushed, but in County Down the rebels succeeded in occupying Saintfield. They were soon dislodged, however, by government forces under the command of Major-General George Nugent. Having burned Saintfield to the ground, Nugent's troops reached Ballynahinch on the following day and proceeded to bombard the town. On the morning of 13 June 1798 the rebels' ammunition ran out and Nugent's army overwhelmed them on Ednavady Hill. No mercy was shown and Nugent later claimed to have killed 300 in the fighting and a further 200 in the pursuit. With the town a smoking ruin and bodies lying unburied in the streets, the rising in County Down was over.

The most important source of information on the United Irishmen and the 1798 rebellion is the 'Rebellion Papers' in the National Archives in Dublin. For an online survey of the Rebellion Papers, see: www.nation-alarchives.ie/topics/rebellion/redpapers.htm. In PRONI there are also numerous items that can be consulted. These include the 'Black Book of the Rebellion of the North of Ireland' (D/272/1), which contains the names of some 200 individuals who were members or suspected to be members of the United Irishmen. There are also lists from 1798–99 of persons confined by order of the government in Belfast, Carrickfergus and the prison ship *Postlethwaite*, and affidavits of United Irishmen (PRONI D/272).

Chapter 5

SEVENTEENTH-CENTURY RECORDS

1602 'Census of Fews'

In 1602 the Irish leader Sir Turlough McHenry O'Neill was granted a pardon by Elizabeth I. During the Plantation of Ulster he was allocated land in Upper Fews. This so-called census is in fact a copy of the pardon which consists of a list of the heads of each household in the Fews and includes the names of the few women who were tenants in their own right. A total of 270 names are recorded and the list has been published in the *County Louth Archaelogical* Journal, vol. VIII (1934). A copy is now available online at: generation13.net/Censusnotebook/pagedex/Fews1.htm.

Fiants of the Tudor sovereigns, 1521–1603

The Irish fiants of the Tudor sovereigns, Henry VIII, Edward VI, Philip and Mary, Elizabeth I, have been called the single most important source for sixteenth-century Irish history. Fiants were the warrants issued to command the drawing up of letters patent, the formal royal letters by which grants of land, official appointments, pardons, etc. were made, but in the Tudor period the drawing up of the actual letters patent was often neglected, and the fiants remained the basic record.

The uniqueness of the information contained in the fiants encouraged the staff in the newly established Public Record Office of Ireland to publish calendars of these fiants. Ingeniously, they got the calendars published as appendices in the steady stream of annual reports published by the office in the years 1857–90 (Reports Nos 11–13, 15–18 of the *Deputy Keeper of the Public Records of Ireland*). The attention of the scholarly world was drawn to the quality of the information available in the fiants by the publication of reprints of these calendars of Irish fiants for the years 1521–1603 by Edmund Burke in 1994. These serve as very adequate substitutes for the original records destroyed in the Public Record Office of Ireland.

When Irish chiefs were granted pardons under the 'surrender and regrant' policy they often listed scores of members of their extended families as well as kerns and gallowglasses (mercenary soldiers), horsemen and yeomen, husbandmen, tenants and even, on occasion, cottiers. Individuals were identified with their full names, often with specific locations.

Calendars of patent rolls from the reigns of James I and Charles I

The patent rolls were the most important records in the chancery archives. On them were enrolled copies of letters patent, which granted Crown lands on lease, surrenders and regrants to Irish lords, royal letters and many other documents of which it was thought necessary to keep a record. A roll generally contains the record of one year.

The original Irish patent rolls were also destroyed in the Public Record Office, Dublin, in 1922. Fortunately, some of the material had been published in calendar form. Printed calendars have survived for the patent rolls of James I and the early part of the reign of Charles I. These contain the names of the native Irish who received grants of land or were pardoned for transgressions committed during the years 1603–33. The calendars also include the names of Scots in Ulster who were given grants of denization to enable them to enjoy the same rights as English subjects. This was particularly important in matters of inheritance. The Revd David Stewart, a Presbyterian minister and a very active local historian, extracted the names of about 1,000 Scots who were recorded as having been granted denization from the printed calendars.

The *Calendar of the Patent Rolls of the Reign of James I* was prepared under the direction of the Irish Record Commission prior to 1830 and was printed before the Commission closed. The Irish Manuscripts Commission published a facsimile of the printed calendar in 1966, but this publication is now out of print. Unfortunately, no personal and place-name index to this calendar has as yet been published.

Muster rolls, 1630s and 1640s

These contain lists of the principal landlords in Ulster, and the names of the men they could assemble in an emergency. They are arranged by county, and district within the county, under the PRONI reference MIC/15A/52 – 53 & 73. See also:

Submission of the Gaelic chiefs, contemporary woodcut by John Derricke, British Library.

County Antrim

- Muster roll, 1630–31, PRONI D/1759/3C/3;
- Muster roll, 1642, PRONI T/3726/2.

County Armagh

- Muster roll, 1631, PRONI T/934.

County Down

- Muster roll for County Down, 1630, PRONI D/1759/3C/1;
- Muster roll for County Down 1642–43, PRONI T/563;
- Muster rolls for Donaghadee, County Down, 1642, PRONI T/3726/2.

County Fermanagh

- Muster roll, 1630, PRONI T/510/2;
- Muster roll, 1631, PRONI T/934.

County Londonderry

- Muster roll, 1620–22, PRONI T/510/2;
- Muster roll, 1630–31, PRONI D/1759/3C/2.

County Tyrone

- Muster roll 1630, PRONI T/458/7;
- Muster roll, 1631, PRONI T/934.

The muster roll for 'The City and Libertyes of Londonderry', c. 1630 is available on the Ulster Ancestry website at: www.ulsterancestry.com/ShowFreePage.php?id=262.

Barony d e Magherboy

Mr. Archdals Tenants on his Churchlands being 1000 Acres the names of his Men & Arms as ffolloweth.

1. William Johnston	swd.
2. William Johnston younger	swd. & P.
3. Richard Packrag	swd. & P.
4. George Waret	swd. & P.
5. William Balls	swd. & P.
6. Symond Johston	Call
7. John Little	)
8. Arch Little	No arms
9. Ralph Wyndstandby	)
10. George Chittock	)
11. Andrew Cockaine	)
12. Alexander Wiggin	)
13. Thomas Wiggin	)
14. Robert Armestrang	)

Extract from muster roll for County Fermanagh copied by Revd T H Steele and available at the PRONI and Fermanagh Divisional Library Enniskillen.

Depositions of 1641 rising

By the 1640s, the number of English and Scottish settlers in Ulster had swelled to some 40,000, ensuring that the north-east of the country was dominated by a Protestant, English-speaking community. The natives, nevertheless, remained a threat. In 1628 Sir Thomas Phillips warned the government that 'it is feared that they will rise upon a sudden and cut the throats of the poor dispersed British'. Rebellion came in October 1641. Soon large parts of Tyrone, Armagh, Cavan, Fermanagh and Down were in rebel hands and by November Leinster had risen and Drogheda was besieged. Protestant settlers were evicted from their lands, farms were burnt and cattle stolen. Local government quickly collapsed which resulted in a breakdown of law and order and a consequent panic throughout Ulster. John Galbraith, travelling from Scotland to Dublin through east Ulster in November 1641, observed: 'the most woeful desolation that was ever in any country on the sudden is to be seen there. Such is the sudden fear and amazement that has seized all sorts of people that they are ready to run into the sea'.

It took nearly a decade to suppress the rebellion. The final event that sealed the Irish's fate came in August 1649, when Oliver Cromwell arrived in Dublin with 3,000 English calvary. Cromwell, fresh from leading the Parliamentary forces to victory over King Charles I, arrived in Ireland with the object of regaining control of Ireland and avenging the colonists who were massacred in 1641. This he did with characteristic ruthlessness; the massacres carried out at Drogheda and Wexford in particular left a bitter legacy. Those lands belonging to Irish insurgents were confiscated and divided out under the supervision of a commission of the revenue established at Carrickfergus under the governor, Colonel Arthur Hill of Hillsborough. The most guilty, including 105 named chief rebels, were executed, banished or transported, while others who had not shown 'constant good affection' to Parliament were subject to various levels of forfeiture and transplantation to Connaught and County Clare.

The depositions of 1641 are the collected accounts of witnesses to the robberies and murders that took place during the rising. In December 1641 and January 1642 eight Protestant clergymen, led by Henry Jones Dean of Kilmore, were empowered to take evidence during town commissions. In 1652, following Cromwell's subjugation of the country a High Court of

Justice was established to collect evidence for the trials of those who had risen against the settlers.

More than 140 depositions relating to the rising of 1641 in County Armagh have survived and are deposited in the library of Trinity College, Dublin. The majority of the witnesses were English settlers and their occupations ranged from 'gentlemen' to 'tanners', 'tailors' and 'inn keepers'. Nevertheless, they named their attackers or those rumoured to have taken part in the rising and the depositions do provide rare documentary evidence of the native Irish families who had once dominated the country.

Extract of 1641 deposition

The examination of John Taylor aged about 30 years, being duly sworn saith, that being an inhabitant of Tandragee, at the beginning of the rebellion, was kept there by force in the said town with many more both English and Scots till about May following.

'But upon the march of the British Army towards Newry, the Irish then in and about Tandragee caused all the prisoners to be gathered together, to the constables house of the said town, from which place they were carried away about a mile to the river, and then was stripped naked, knocked on the head, and thrown into the river, all both men and women and children. The chief actors in this bloody massacre was, Colonel Edmond Ogge O'Hanlon, Governor at Tandragee, and his 3 brothers Patt Ogge O'Hanlon, since slain, Ardell Oge O'Hanlon, since died likewise, and Furdorragh O'Hanlon with their soldiers.

And that William McToole was, as this examinant heard, one of the actors; the clothes of the murdered being brought to his house, the rest of them, and there was divided . . .' *Taken before us 8 June 1653, George Rawden, Tobias Norrice.*

Copies of the 1641 Depositions are available at the PRONI, reference T/2706/8 and MIC/8/1. Depositions relating to County Armagh are also available in a bound transcript edition at the Armagh County Museum.

Books of Survey and Distribution

These were compiled around 1680 as a result of the wars of the mid-seventeenth century when the English government needed reliable information on land ownership throughout Ireland to carry out its policies of land

Woodcut depicting the 1641 rising, London, 1655, British Library.

ownership and land distribution throughout Ireland. The Books of Survey and Distribution are laid out on a barony and parish basis and include a record of land ownership before the Cromwellian and Williamite confiscations as well as the names of the individuals to whom the land was distributed. They were used to impose the acreable rent called the Quit Rent, which was payable yearly on lands granted under the terms of the Acts of Settlement and Explanation. A fire in 1711 in the Surveyors and Auditor General Office destroyed the office copies of the Books of Survey and Distribution, but fortunately duplicate copies have survived. A set can be found in the Annesley Papers PRONI reference MIC/532/1–23.

Civil Survey of Ireland

Sir William Petty's Civil Survey of Ireland, compiled between 1655 and 1667, contains lists of the principal landlords of each townland as well as their predecessor before the Cromwellian confiscations of 1641. It contains a great deal of topographical information arranged by county, barony, parish and townland. Unfortunately, very little of this survey survives, although County Londonderry and County Tyrone are available under PRONI reference T/371.

Census of Ireland, *c.* 1659

The so-called census of 1659 was probably made by Sir William Petty's surveyors. Petty, described by Samuel Pepys as 'the most intelligent man I know', arrived in Ireland in 1652 as physician-general to Cromwell's armies. He soon abandoned medicine in order to concentrate on cartography, surveying and economics and was made responsible for mapping all the 2,800,000 acres of land confiscated after the Cromwellian victory in Ireland. It was the first systematic survey of Ireland, requiring 1,000 assistants, and in many ways was a forerunner of the Ordnance Survey. The census of 1659 contains only the names of those with title to land (tituladoes) and the total number of English and Irish resident in each townland (Scots were usually counted with English). There are five counties not covered: Cavan, Galway, Mayo, Tyrone and Wicklow. An edition of the census by Seamus Pender was published in 1939 by the Stationery Office, Dublin, on behalf of the Irish Manuscripts Commission. This includes a breakdown of the figures for each county and an index of both personal names and place names. You can consult the following at PRONI:

County Armagh

- 1659 Census MIC/15A/72.

County Antrim

- 1659 Census MIC/15A/72.

County Fermanagh

- 1659 Census T/808/15064.

County Londonderry

- 1659 Census MIC/15A/82.

The following extract is taken from Seamus Pender's edition of the 1659 census published by the Irish Manuscripts Commission.

LONDONDERRY CITTY AND COUNTY, 1659

Parishes	Streets	Number of People	Tituladoes Nanes	Eng & Scots	Irish
Templemore	Silver Streete	52	Col George Gorges, Samuel Hill Esq, Henry Osborne, and John Plunkett, gents, John McKenny John Burnside, and James Lenox merchants	34	18
	Diamond Street	14	James Hobson, John Craig and Thomas Moncreife merchant	10	4

Poll Tax returns, 1660

The Poll Tax Rolls list the people who paid a tax levied on every person over 12 years of age. According to an Ordinance of the General Convention dated 24 April 1660, all persons of the ranks and degrees therein mentioned should pay the respective sums of money appointed and that 'every person above the age of fifteen years of either sex . . . under the degree or quality of yeoman, or farmer yeoman, or farmer's wife or widow shall pay twelve pence'. They give detailed facts about individuals that are quite unique in surviving seventeenth-century records. See the following:

County Armagh

- 1660 Poll Tax returns PRONI MIC/15A/74; RCB Ms Libr.48

County Down

- 1660 Poll Tax returns PRONI MIC/15A/72;
- 1698 Poll Tax returns, Newry and Mourne PRONI T/1046.

County Fermanagh

- 1660 Poll Tax returns PRONI MIC/15A/80.

County Londonderry

- 1669 Poll Tax returns PRONI MIC/15A/82.

County Tyrone

- 1696 and 1698 Manuscript notes and details of Poll Tax payments PRONI T/808/15095.

Hearth-money rolls, 1666

Arranged by county and parish, they list the name of the householder and the number of hearths on which he was taxed at the rate of 2s on every hearth or fireplace. Hearth money was introduced into Ireland in 1662. The Irish House of Commons, in appreciation of His Majesty's 'great and abundant goodness by his freely parting with almost all the great forfeitures devolved to the Crown', proposed that 'the late precedent in England was worthy of imitation and that 2/- per annum be paid out of all chimneys, stoves and hearths'. The tax was to be paid by the tenant of every house, with the exception only of people not able to get their living by work, and widows falling below certain property qualifications. Attempts were made to avoid payment and in 1665 fines were imposed for concealment of hearths. The tax was levied twice a year, at Lady Day (25 March, the official start of the year until 1752) and Michaelmas (29 September, the feast of Michael the Archangel). During this time the tax was the government's major source of revenue. Its unpopularity led to its abolition in England and Wales after the Glorious Revolution of 1688. In Ireland it continued to be levied until the Act of Union in 1800. The original hearth-money rolls were destroyed in the Four Courts in 1922. Fortunately, the Presbyterian Historical Society of Ireland had preserved copies of the rolls. See the following:

County Antrim

- 1669 Hearth Money Roll T/307.

County Armagh

* 1664 Hearth Money Roll T/604.

County Fermanagh

* 1665–66 Hearth Money Roll T/808/15066.

County Londonderry

* 1663 Hearth Money Roll T/307.

County Tyrone

* 1664 Hearth Money Roll T/283/D/2;
* 1666 Hearth Money Roll T/307.

Subsidy rolls, 1630s, 1660s

The subsidy rolls list the nobility, clergy and laity who paid a grant in aid to the King, for example, those who possessed sufficient property to be liable to payment of the subsidies which then formed the chief manner of direct taxation. The lists in this case, therefore, are of the better class citizens. They include the name and the parish of the person and some-times the amount paid and the status of the person. An index to the names of persons listed in the 1663 Subsidy Roll is available on the shelves of the Public Search Room at PRONI and a copy is available under reference T/307. Copies are also available at the National Library of Ireland (Ms 9584/5) and the National Archives of Ireland (M 2745). The following are of particular interest:

County Antrim

* 1666 Subsidy Roll T/808/14889.

County Armagh

- 1634 Subsidy Roll NA M.2471; Representative Church Body Ms Libr 48;

- A Subsidy Roll for the Portadown area is also available for 1634, see PRONI T/281/7.

County Down

- 1663 Subsidy Roll PRONI T/307; NA M.2745; NL Ms 9584 with index 9585.

County Fermanagh

- 1662 Subsidy Roll PRONI T/808/15068; NL Ms 9583;

- 1663 (Enniskillen town only).

County Tyrone

- 1664 Subsidy Roll PRONI T/283/D/1; NL Ms 9583;

- 1665, 1668, Subsidy Rolls held by Armagh Museum, n. 12 p. 206;

- 1667, 1668 Subsidy Rolls held by National Archives, M.2470.

The Franciscan Petition Lists, 1670–71

Although the hearth-money rolls remain the main genealogical source for the seventeenth century, the Franciscan Petition Lists should not be neglected for they contain the names of individuals in County Armagh that are not found in any other archive.

The records themselves relate to a dispute between the Franciscans and the Dominicans which had its origins in the 1640s. During the seventeenth century the Dominicans, as a result of their increasing membership, had come into conflict with the Franciscans over their respective rights over the collection of alms or donations. The majority of the clergy and laity in Ulster supported the Franciscans and elected members of the congregation to represent their views to the Lord Primate Oliver Plunkett.

The Franciscan Petition Lists, therefore, contain the names of the clergy, gentry and parishioners of various townlands and parishes within the Armagh Diocese.

Extract from the petition for the parish of Creggan

Here followeth the names of the parishioners of parish of Creggan, by their one consent and humble request drawen, against certaine Dominicans pretending to intrude uniustly upon them, and severall others, commonly begging at their alters to their xame and ungability etc. being unable (God help them) to maintaine their one clergy booth secular and regular, as their predecesors did, which is enough for them, I pray God they may doe it.

Manutius Conneus curatus etc.

Pattr: Grome O Quine	Bryan O Quine
Neall McShane	Thorlaugh McGoirk
Edd McShane	John McGoirk
Owen McShane	Pattrick McGille
Caheer McShane	Edmond McShane
Phelim McShane	Thorlough McGoork
Cormuck O Quine	Hugh O Quine
Pattr: O Quine	Pattr: Callaghan
Bryan O Quine	Cormuck Callaghan
Eneas Quine	Thomas Callaghan
Bryan McCardell	Edd Donnelly
James McCardell	Bryan Callaghan.

The complete list for the Diocese of Armagh has been published by Patrick J Campbell in *Seanchas Ardmhacha*, Journal of the Armagh Diocesan Historical Society, vol. 15, no. 1 (1992).

Names of those attainted by James II, 1689

The accession of James II in 1685 brought about a sudden and fundamental change of policy in favour of his Catholic supporters. Having been ejected from the throne in England, James found refuge in Ireland, still controlled for the most part by his supporters. His Irish Parliament of 1689 was dominated by the Old English, which reversed the seventeenth-century land settlements. In 1689 an 'Act for the Attainder of Diverts Rebels, and for Preserving the Interest of Loyal Subjects' was also passed in the Irish Parliament. It listed the names of Irish Protestants considered by the government of James II to be disloyal to the King. Most of those listed were members of the landed gentry or freeholders. The names of those attainted (i.e., found guilty of treason) were published in *The State of the Protestants of Ireland under the late King James's Government* by William King (Dublin, 1713). A photocopy of the relevant pages from this book is available on the open shelves of the Public Search Room at PRONI. A list of names of Protestants in County Armagh attained in 1689 by James II can be found at PRONI reference T/808/14985.

Siege of Derry, 1689, Mansell Collection.

Williamite War and Siege of Londonderry, 1689

After the Glorious Revolution in 1688, most settlers in Ulster came out in favour of King William. In December 1688 thirteen Apprentices closed the city gates against a Jacobite force. In the spring of 1689, James II proceeded against the city which by now had become the focus of Protestant defiance of his authority in the north of Ireland. The subsequent siege lasted from 16 April to 1 August 1689 by which time the inhabitants were reduced to eating mice, rats and dogs fattened on human corpses. The siege was finally ended when a Williamite relief force broke through the Jacobite boom on the River Foyle. The siege is still a central part of Ulster legend and is commemorated twice a year: on 12 August for the relief of the city and in December with the closing of the city gates by the Apprentice Boys.

After James II had been overthrown from his throne in the 'Glorious Revolution' much of Ireland remained loyal under the Catholic administration of Richard Talbot, Earl of Tyrconnell. James landed in Ireland in March 1689 with a French army and after failing to capture Londonderry and Enniskillen managed to prevent the advance of the Williamite forces under Marshal Schomberg. By June 1691 William himself had taken charge of the armed forces in Ireland, made up of English, Dutch, French Huguenots and

Danes as well as six Ulster regiments. On 1 July William defeated the Jacobite forces at the Boyne, giving him control of Dublin and the eastern half of the country. Muster and Connaught were finally secured by victory at the battle of Aughrim on 12 July 1691.

For information on those who were involved in the siege of Derry and events during the Williamite War in general, the best single source is W R Young, *Fighters of Derry, Their Deeds and Descendents, Being a Chronicle of Events in Ireland during the Revolutionary Period, 1688–91* (London, 1932). This lists the names of some 1,660 individuals who defended Derry or were associated with William of Orange; for many of them brief biographical sketches are also provided. Young has also compiled a list of 352 Jacobites, again with biographical sketches of many of them. *Illustrations Historical and Genealogical of King James II's Irish Army List* (1689), by John D'Alton, contains information on those who served the Jacobite cause. The second edition was published in 1861.

Regiments of infantry

Alexander, Earl of Antrim

Captains	Lieutenants	Ensigns
The Colonel.	Archibald M'Donnell	Randall M'Donnell
Mark Talbot,		
Lieut-Col.	Denis Callaghan	———Makay
James Wogan,		
Major	Francis Moore.	Con. O'Rourke.
Lord Iniskillen	{Eneas McDonnell	
	{John O'Neale.	Francis O'Neille
Hugh O'Neill	Bryan O'Neale.	Augustin McDonnell.
Edmund Reilly	Bryan Magrath	Fran. Reilly
Manus O'Donnell	Bryan O'Neill	John O'Cahan

Extract taken from *King James II's Irish Army List* (1689) by John D'Alton.

Chapter 6

THE PLANTATION
OF ULSTER

At the closing years of the Elizabethan period, a prolonged war aimed at bringing the Ulster chiefs into submission had laid waste large tracts of the country. Upon the surrender of Hugh O'Neill, Earl of Tyrone, the chief general of the Irish forces, Ulster came under English law. The new King, James I, at first took a conciliatory approach. The Ulster chiefs retained their titles and were recognised as landowners of huge areas. The generous pardon infuriated those who had fought for the Crown in the long wars in Ulster. One of them complained: 'I have lived to see that damnable rebel Tyrone brought to England, honoured, and well liked . . . I adventured perils by sea and land, was near starving, ate horse flesh in Munster, and all to quell that man, who now smileth in peace at those who did hazard their lives to destroy him.'

The new English officials, however, undermined the Ulster chiefs at every opportunity. The lord deputy, Sir Arthur Chichester, and the attorney general, Sir John Davies, eroded the Earl of Tyrone's authority to the extent that, in the lord deputy's words, 'now the law of England, and the Ministers thereof, were shakles and handlocks unto him, and the garrisons planted in his country were as pricks in his side'. This policy worked even better than the English officials could have hoped. In 1607, Tyrone, Rory O'Donnell, Earl of Tyrconnell, and Cuconnacht Maguire, Lord of Fermanagh, together with their followers, wives and families, left Ulster and went to the continent, an event now remembered as the 'Flight of the Earls'.

The departure of so many of the principal chiefs and landowners offered the English government an excellent opportunity for a change of policy that would end all possibility of future trouble in Ulster. The lord deputy

Flight of the Earls, *by Thomas Ryan.*

wrote to James I in September 1607: 'If his Majesty will, during their absence, assume the countries into his possession, divide the lands amongst the inhabitants . . . and will bestow the rest upon servitors and men of worth here, and withal bring in colonies of civil people of England and Scotland . . . the country will ever after be happily settled.' It was the perfect time to take such an initiative, for 'the whole realm, and especially the fugitive countries, are more utterly depopulated and poor than ever before for many hundred years'.

A revolt in April 1608 led by the formerly pro-English Sir Cahir O'Doherty in north-west Ulster underlined the importance of settling the area and provided the opportunity for extending the area of confiscated land designated for plantation. The King's enthusiasm for the venture had already been kindled by the success of pioneering settlements in County Down. Shortly before the Plantation, two Scottish adventurers named Montgomery and Hamilton had established a community of lowland Scots in County Down which were to form the bridgehead through which Scots settlers spread out into Ulster for much of the seventeenth century. With surnames such as Calderwood, Agnew, Adair, Cunningham, Shaw and Maxwell, they arrived to find the country 'more wasted than America (when the Spanish landed there)', and between Donaghadee and Newtown 'thirty cabins could not be found, nor any stone walls, but ruined, roofless churches, and a few vaults at Grey Abbey, and a stump of an old castle at Newtown'.

County Antrim too had a strong Scottish presence. Immigration from Scotland had been fairly continuous for centuries before 1609. In 1399 the heiress of the Norman lordship in eastern Antrim married John Mor MacDonnell, the Lord of the Isles. Antrim was absorbed in the MacDonnell kingdom and this situation lasted until the fifteenth century. More recently, a strong English presence had established itself in South Antrim under Sir Arthur Chichester, a Devon man, who was to be responsible for the new plantation scheme. He was determined to lead the way by setting a good example on his own lands in and around Belfast. Many of his supporters secured estates to the south of Belfast, particularly in the Malone area, ensuring that north Down was noticeably English in character. In 1635 an English traveller recorded that Chichester's house was 'the glory and beauty of the town'. No mention is made of the town itself except that 'many Cheshire and Lancashire men were planted in the neighbourhood by Mr. Arthur Hill, son of Sir Moyses Hill'. Belfast itself was peopled with Devonshire men, and a number of Scots settlers.

Planning for the Ulster Plantation got underway shortly after the 'Flight of the Earls' in September 1607. The initial 1608 survey of confiscated lands was discovered to be so imperfect that a second survey was required during 1609. Both Down and Antrim, with a strong Scottish presence already, were not included in the scheme. County Monaghan was the only other entire county of Ulster to be excluded from the official scheme. In 1591 land tenure in Monaghan had been anglicised through the transference of extensive Church lands to English servitors and by granting land to loyal Irish landowners.

The 'Printed Book' of conditions for successful applicants for Ulster land was published in London in April 1610. Much of the land was confiscated in the six Ulster counties of Armagh, Cavan, Donegal, Coleraine (later Londonderrry), Fermanagh and Tyrone. Undertakers had to be English or Scottish who had taken the Oath of Surpremacy – that is Protestants – and who were to pay rent of £5 6s 8d to the King for every 1,000 acres. They were assigned the lands at favourable terms. Proportions allocated varied from 2,000, 1,500 to 1,000 acres. They were expected to clear their new estates completely of native Irish inhabitants. Undertakers were also expected to settle 24 British males per 1,000 acres of lands granted. The undertakers who were granted the largest proportions, 2,000 acres, were expected to build a castle on their lands, whereas stone bawns were required to be built by undertakers with smaller proportions. Building and settlement had to be completed within three years.

Some native Irish were exempt from the Plantation, the most notable being Conor Roe Maguire in east Fermanagh, Sir Tourlough MacHenry O'Neill of the Fews, and in Armagh and Tyrone, the heirs of Sir Henry Og O Neill, who had been killed in the campaign to suppress O'Doherty's revolt. A total of 280 Irish obtained Plantation land grants, which amounted to about 20 per cent of the planted counties. They were given reduced holdings, often shifted to place them under local servitor supervision, and forbidden to buy additional land. Some received life grants only. On the eve of the Plantation Sir Toby Caulfied reported that there was 'not a more discontented people in Europe'.

The new Plantation's chances of success were considerably boosted when the Crown secured the support of the city of London in the enterprise. In return James I granted the London Companies not only all of County Coleraine, but also the barony of Loughinsholin, detached from Tyrone, together with Culmore and the towns of Coleraine and Derry.

Settlers began to arrive in Ulster as the Plantation scheme gradually took shape. They levelled the forests and devoted themselves to arable farming, built towns and villages of neat timber framed houses and thatched or slated stone cottages, established markets, churches and schools. The English tenants who were attracted to Ulster came from the northern borders of England or had gone to Ireland to work temporarily on the building programme of the Plantation but had been inveigled to stay on as tenants by landlords desperate to fulfil the tenancy terms of their agreements. The Welsh too settled in considerable numbers in Dungannon, County Tyrone and in County Donegal. The Scots came in greatest numbers from the eight counties that lay either along the border with England, or up the west coast of Scotland. Most came from south-west Scotland, Lanark, Renfew and Sterlingshire where land was hard to come by and lairds evicted tenants unable to make the down payments required under the 'feuing' land-letting system. Surviving records suggest that Tyrone and Fermanagh attracted relatively large numbers of settlers from the Border counties. The most common surnames were Johnson, Armstrong, Elliot, Graham and Beatty. In Donegal, Londonderry, Cavan and Armagh, the majority of settlers came from the western Lowlands.

After a slow beginning, during the 1630s a second wave of Scots was attracted to Ulster for economic reasons. Many were living in poverty in their home areas as an expanding population, rising prices and increased unemployment led to serious economic problems in Scotland, particularly in the 1630s. Migration to Ireland offered the possibility of immediate escape from dire poverty and the prospect of future prosperity. Sir William Brereton, an Englishman travelling through Ayrshire in 1634, wrote:

'Above ten thousand persons have, within two last years past, left the country wherein they lived . . . and are gone for Ireland. They have come by one hundred in company through the town, and three hundred have gone on hence together, shipped for Ireland at one tide . . .'.

The records

The government commissioned four surveys between 1611 and 1622 to investigate the progress being made in the Ulster Plantation. These surveys are located as follows:

Dunluce Castle, The Scenery and Antiquities of Ireland, *drawn by W H Bartlett (1841)*.

- 1611 – survey carried out by Sir George Carew, *Calendar of the Carew Manuscripts, 1603–24*, pp. 68–69, 75–79, 220–51;

- 1613 – survey carried out by Sir Josias Bodley, Historical Manuscripts Commission, *Hastings Mss, iv* (London, 1947), pp. 159–92;

- 1618–19 – survey carried out by Captain Nicholas Pynnar. The findings are held by Trinity College, Dublin, F.1.19. The survey is printed in full in G Hill, *Historical Account of the Plantation of Ulster* (Belfast, 1877);

- 1622 – survey carried out by commissioners appointed by the government. The official reports for each county were published as follows:

Armagh: V Treadwell in *Ulster Journal of Archaeology*, 3rd series, 23 (1960)
Cavan: P O Gallachair in *Breifne*, vol. 1 (1958)
Donegal: V Treadwell in *Donegal Annual*, vol. 2 (1951–54), vol. 3 (1954–57)
Fermanagh: P O Gallachair in *Clogher Record*, vol. 2 (1958)
Londonderry: *Calendar of the State Papers Relating to Ireland*, 1615–25
Tyrone: V Treadwell in *Ulster Journal of Archaeology*, 3rd series, vol. 27 (1964).

In December 2006, the Irish Manuscripts Commission published Victor Treadwell's book which contains the papers of the commission of enquiry sent to Ireland in 1622. This volume details the daily functioning of the commission and has substantial indices of persons and places.

There is also a significant amount of original documentation relating to the 1622 survey in the National Library of Ireland under Ms Manuscripts under DD/M. This material includes many of the original certificates presented by the undertakers or their agents. Names of tenants are provided as well as information on the buildings on the estate and who had built them.

State papers concerning Ireland are preserved in the National Archives, London under SP/63. Microfilm copies of the original state papers, covering the period 1509–1782, can be found in PRONI (MIC/223).

Plantation records of the London Companies

In 1609 the city of London was invited to undertake the corporate plantation of Derry and Tyrone. It was an acknowledgement by the government that the scheme was attracting settlers to O'Cahan country, and that holding the strategically important towns of Derry and Coleraine would likely be beyond the resources of the average adventurer. After difficult negotiations the government granted to the City practically the whole of the county of Coleraine (later Londonderry) and the Tyrone barony of Loughinsholin. In return the corporation undertook to spend £20,000, and within 2 years to build 200 houses in Derry and 100 in Coleraine. A new body was also created to supervise and manage the running of the Plantation, to be called 'The Society of the Governor and Assistants, London, of the New Plantation of Ulster, within the Realm of Ireland', known later as The Honourable The Irish Society.

In total fifty-five London Companies were ordered to contribute to the Plantation, at rates determined according to their wealth and prestige. Although prison and fines were used by the government to encourage the payment of arrears, some Londoners preferred these punishments to participation in the scheme. Some of the unwillingness to pay up may have been due to the fact that the Crown delayed in formalising title to the lands: to remedy this, the Charter of Londonderry was ratified in March 1613. The Charter created the county of Londonderry – so named to emphasise the connection with London – by combining the former county of Coleraine, most of the barony of Loughinsholin detached from Tyrone, Derry and its north-west liberties and Coleraine and its north-east liberties.

The Irish Society's and London Companies' interest in their Ulster estates lasted until the land-purchase legislation at the end of the nine-

Relief of Derry,
by William
Sadler, Ulster
Museum.

teenth and twentieth centuries. John Towgood left an account of his visit to the Company lands at and near Newtownlimavady in 1820 (PRONI reference MIC/9B/Reel 17):

Saturday, 1st April. We proceeded after breakfast on a further view of the estate in company with Mr J Given, Junior, in the course of the day we entered, as we had before done, many very wretched hovels, called cabins. The following picture will apply with variations to most of them. On entering the cabin, by a door through which smoke is perhaps issuing at the time, you observe a bog peat fire, around which is a group of boys and girls as ragged as possible, and all without shoes or stockings, sometimes a large pig crosses the cabin without ceremony, or a small one is lying by the fire with its nose close to the toes of the children; perhaps an old man is seen or woman, the grandfather or grandmother of the family with a baby in her lap – two of three stout girls spinning flax, the spinning wheels making a whirring noise, like the humming of bees; a dog lying at his length in the chimney corner perhaps a goose hatching her eggs under the dresser and all this in a small cabin full of smoke, an earth floor, a heap of potatoes in one corner and a heap of peat turf in another, sometimes a cow and sometimes a horse occupy the corner.

The records relate to the administration of their extensive estates and include rentals, title deeds, maps and correspondence. The originals of many of the Irish Society and London Companies' records are held by the Corporation of London Record Office, the Guidhall Library in London, or by the Companies themselves. PRONI holds microfilm copies of much of this material. In the 1980s the Drapers' Company deposited records relating to its County Londonderry Estates at PRONI. This archive, consisting of about 500 volumes and about 15,000 documents, is now fully catalogued, PRONI reference number D/3632. PRONI also holds records of the smaller companies – the Barber Surgeons (associated in the 1613 division of estates with the Ironmongers), the Cordwainers (associated with the Goldsmiths), Cutlers and Joiners (associated with the Salters), the Wax Chandlers (associated with the Haberdashers) and Weavers (associated with the Vinters).

In addition to the records of the individual companies, PRONI has a wide range of records relating to the various individuals who acquired land through or from these companies.

The *Guide to Records of the Irish Society and the London Companies* has been published by PRONI. It is arranged alphabetically by Company with a final section on the Irish Society.

Chapter 7

CHURCH RECORDS

In the early nineteenth century the three major denominations, Roman Catholic, Anglican and Presbyterian, between them accounted for all but a very small proportion of the Northern Irish population. They were unevenly distributed across the country. In 1861 Catholics made up a minority of the population in four Ulster counties (Antrim, Armagh, Down and Londonderry) as well as in the towns of Belfast and Carrickfergus. In two other Ulster counties, Fermanagh and Tyrone, they accounted for not much more than half the population. In the counties of Antrim and Down, and in Belfast and Carrickfergus, Presbyterians were the largest single religious group, while they were also well represented in County Londonderry. Irish Anglicans were more dispersed across Northern Ireland and tended to be over represented among the landowner class.

The spiritual capital of Ireland is the city of Armagh. St Patrick called Armagh 'my sweet hill' and persuaded Daire the local chieftain to grant him the hilltop site where he built his stone church and where the Anglican cathedral now stands. After the foundation of Partick's church in 445 AD other churches, colleges and schools flourished making Armagh one of the great centres of learning in Europe. From the eighth century the abbot-bishops of Armagh pressed their claims as the inheritors of St Patick's mission, and in 1004 this primacy was recognised by Brian Boru as High King of Ireland. The religious foundations at Armagh attracted the Vikings during the ninth century and they frequently attacked and destroyed the monastic settlements in the city before Brian Boru, High King of Ireland, won a decisive battle over them at Clontarf in 1014. Boru, his son and nephew were killed on the battlefield and their bodies are said to be buried on the north side of Armagh cathedral.

The monastic settlements in Armagh were frequently at the mercy of opposing Irish forces as the O'Neills established their dominance over their neighbours. The Anglo-Normans during the later twelfth century attacked

St Patrick's Catholic Cathedral, PRONI, Allison Collection, A/1/3/22.

and plundered Armagh on numerous occasions, and during the sixteenth century and early seventeenth century the city was sacked by opposing Irish and English forces. With the Plantation of Ulster, Armagh re-established itself as the ecclesiastic capital of Ireland and the Anglican Primate Richard Robinson, appointed in 1765, was responsible for many of the fine buildings that can be seen in Armagh today. Nowadays it is the seat of both Protestant and Catholic archbishops and the city is dominated by the Anglican and Roman Catholic cathedrals.

By the beginning of the eighteenth century the Anglican Church had acquired a virtual monopoly of power in Ireland. One of the earliest orders in the Belfast Corporation related to the enforcing the Act of Uniformity in Belfast:

October 15, 1615. It was Ordered that every freeman and other inhabitant within the Corporation, of the age of eighteen years or above, that shall be absent from Church or other place appointed for common prayer upon the 'Sabbath' or any other day appointed to be kept holy by the Laws or Statutes of this Realm without reasonable cause, shall for every default forfeit to the use of the Corporation as followeth, viz:- Every householder 5 shillings; every woman that is married 2 shillings and 6 pence; every servant man or woman one shilling; every child Ten pence, to be levied by distress by the church-wardens of the Parish of Shankhill out of the goods and chattels of every offender who is a householder; and all other forfeitures for the married women, servants, and children to be levied out of the goods of the husbands, fathers, mothers, and masters of the said offenders.

The Church of Ireland also had important civic responsibilities. The parish vestry was used to collect the rates for lighting, paving and watching the town until the middle of the nineteenth century.

William Makepeace Thackeray, when visiting the town in the early 1840s, noted the number of churches in Belfast:

> The stranger cannot fail to be struck (and haply a little frightened) by the great number of meeting houses that decorate the town, and give evidence of great sermonizing on Sundays. These buildings do not affect the Gothic, like many of the meagre edifices of the Established and the Roman Catholic churches, but have a physiognomy of their own – a thick-set citizen look.

It is ironic, therefore, that by the end of that century the city still did not have a cathedral. With the appointment of Henry Stewart O'Hara as Vicar of Belfast in 1894 the idea of building a cathedral gathered strength and it was decided to build it on the site of St Anne's Church, founded in 1776 by the first Marquis of Donegall. The foundation stone was laid on 6 September 1899 by the Countess of Shaftesbury but it was not until 1981 that the final phase of the cathedral was completed.

Presbyterianism came to Northern Ireland from Scotland with the first Plantation of Ulster during the early seventeenth century. Despite their prominent role in the dynastic wars of the seventeenth century and the crucial role they played in defending Derry and Enniskillen for William of Orange, legislation was enacted against Presbyterians and Dissenters in order to reduce them to the same impotent state as Irish Catholics. In 1704 the Test Act was passed which required all office holders in Ireland to take the sacrament of the Anglican Church. Presbyterian ministers had now no official standing and marriages performed by them were null and void. Presbyterians and other Dissenters could not now serve in the Army, the militia, the civil service, the municipal corporations, the teaching profession or the commission of the peace. At Belfast the entire Corporation was expelled, and Londonderry lost ten of its twelve aldermen.

Their freedom of action was severely curtailed by the penal laws so that it was technically illegal for Presbyterian ministers to perform marriages of members of their congregation until 1782 and it was not until 1845 that they could legally marry a Presbyterian and a member of the Church of Ireland. The result was that from the early years of the eighteenth century, thousands of Presbyterians from the north of Ireland emigrated to the colonies of British North America, first to New England and then in much larger numbers to Pennsylvania. From the east coast of America they went southwards through the Great Valley, east of the Appalachian Mountains, into the Shenandoah Valley of Virginia and on to the Piedmont region of North and South Carolina. They spearheaded the first thrusts through the Appalachians into Western Pennsylvania, Kentucky and Tennessee; theirs were among the first settlements in Ohio, Illinois and Indiana. From these early pioneers there sprang some of the most eminent names in American history: Andrew Jackson, John C Calhoun, James K Polk and Woodrow Wilson.

Presbyterians remained the largest single religious group in the counties of Antrim and Down, and in Belfast and Carrickfergus, while they were also well represented in County Londonderry. By the end of the eighteenth century the population of Belfast was predominantly Presbyterian. Many Presbyterians were deeply implicated in the United Irish movement. Inspired by the revolutions in America and in France and the publication of Paine's *The Rights of Man*, the United Irishmen sought parliamentary reform and the removal of English control over Irish affairs. The 1798 rising in counties of Antrim and Down quickly ended in disaster. By the middle of the nineteenth century the leading Presbyterian cleric Dr Henry Cooke played a major role in weaning the Presbyterians of Ulster away from their old alliance with the Liberals and Catholics against the Anglican establishment, and substituting a new alliance with the Unionist Episcopalians against the Catholics.

After the Treaty of Limerick in 1691 the Irish Parliament, filled with Protestant landowners and controlled from England, enacted a penal code that secured and enlarged the landlords' holdings and degraded and impoverished the Irish Catholics. As a result of these harsh laws, Catholics could neither teach their children nor send them abroad; persons of property could not enter into mixed marriages; Catholic property was inherited equally among the sons unless one was a Protestant, in which case he received all; a Catholic could not possess arms or a horse worth more than £5; Catholics could not hold leases for more than thirty-one years, and they could not make a profit greater than a third of their rent.

The hierarchy of the Catholic Church was banished or suppressed, and Catholics could not hold seats in the Irish Parliament, hold public office, vote or practise law. Had the laws been ruthlessly put into effect there would soon have been an end to the organised practice of Catholicism. Instead, the laws were sporadically enforced in the seventeenth century and largely ignored in the eighteenth century. The laws affecting property were the most stringently executed, so that most of those Catholic families that owned land eventually became Protestant. Other Catholics conformed in order to practise at the bar or to become solicitors. The social and economic effects of the penal codes on the other hand must have been

*Saintfield
Presbyterian
church, Ulster
Folk and
Transport
Museum,
WAG/3048.*

considerable. Family life was disrupted in many ways: Catholic fathers were estranged from Protestant heirs; bitter disputes were caused by the activities of 'discoverers' within the family. As the Catholic landed class diminished in numbers and influence they were more and more cut off from the social life of the countryside. Uncertainty of tenure discouraged investment in land improvement and led to the cutting of timber for immediate profit. Catholics found a profitable field in trade, and many made fortunes in the seaport towns.

For much of its early history Belfast was a major centre of Protestantism in Ireland. It was recorded in 1707 that there were not 'above seven Papists (in the town) and . . . not above 150 Papists in the whole Barony'. In Belfast by the early part of the eighteenth century there was no resident priest or any church, Derriaghy or Hannahstown being the nearest location for both. Tradition has it that mass was celebrated in the open air at Friar's Bush. It was not until 1784 that the town's first official Catholic chapel was opened in Crooked (now Chapel) Lane. There was a subscription from Protestants of £84 towards its construction. By the early years of the nineteenth century Catholics formed about one-sixth of the population of Belfast, the majority of them located in the area close to the chapel in Crooked Lane. As numbers grew a second church, St Patrick's, was opened on Donegal Street in 1815. 'There are two Roman Catholic Chapels in this town numerous attended', recorded one of the earliest histories of the town published in 1823. 'Before these were built the number of Roman Catholics in Belfast was extremely inconsiderable, mass having been celebrated in the open air at the old grave-yard in Malone, called Friars Bush, and afterwards in a small waste house in Castle Street.'

The Catholic population of Belfast rose rapidly during the nineteenth century. The Industrial Revolution, which was largely confined to north-east Ulster, drew into Belfast vast numbers of workers from Catholic areas in the west and south. By the middle of the nineteenth century the Catholic population was 35 per cent. After the Famine the process was greatly accelerated until today the Catholic proportion of the population of the city is much greater than for the eastern half of Ulster generally. The Catholic cathedral, St Malachy's Church, was built during the early 1840s. An impressive building constructed in dark-red brick, it has slender octagonal corner turrets and a studded Tudor entrance door. Although the church had no bell tower, a bell was hung in the left-hand turret until Dunville's distillery nearby complained that the tolling of the bell 'interfered with the satisfactory maturing of the whiskey'.

William Makepeace Thackeray noted that the religious divisions within the town had a profound impact on local politics:

The three churches are here pretty equally balanced – Presbyterians 25,000, Catholics 20,000, Episcopalians 17,000: each party has two or more newspaper organs; and the wars between them are dire and unceasing, as the reader may imagine. For whereas, in other parts of Ireland where Catholics and Episcopalians prevail, and the Presbyterian body is too small, each party has but one opponent to belabour; here, the Ulster population, whatever may be his way of thinking, has two enemies on whom he may exercise his eloquence: and in this triangular duel all do their duty nobly.

As Belfast's population grew clashes between the different religious groups became an increasing feature of life in the town. Sectarian rivalry manifested itself in waves of rioting beginning with a clash on 12 July 1813 and continuing throughout the nineteenth and twentieth centuries. Polling day battles in 1832, 1835 and 1841 had become by 1857 serious rioting that lasted for days or weeks. Various constitutional crises during the nineteenth century only exasperated sectarianism within Belfast. Daniel O'Connell's campaign for Catholic Emancipation during the 1820s and his Repeal Movement of the 1840s held little appeal for Belfast Protestants. In 1844, a German traveller to Ireland, J G Kohl, remarked that O'Connell tended to avoid the town of Belfast during his tours of Ireland. Kohl was informed of one particular incident during his visit to Belfast:

I was told at Belfast that the great musician Liszt had the misfortune to be taken for O'Connell in the neighbourhood of that city, and was very near undergoing something extremely disagreeable that was intended for the agitator. As Liszt approached from Newry, in a handsome chaise drawn by four horses, and it was rumoured that the carriage contained a celebrated man, some of the Presbyterian rabble imagined it was O'Connell. They stopped the carriage, cut the traces, and compelled the eminent pianist to dismount, in order that they might wreak their anger against him in Irish fashion. They merely wished to duck him in a neighbouring pond, and then to advise him to return to his carriage, and to be off to the south of Ireland. It was some time before they discovered that, instead of the well-fed, old O'Connell, a young artist had fallen into their hands.

The records

One of the most important collections held in the Public Record Office are the Church records and these are an obvious source for family historians. Of particular interest to anyone tracing their family tree are the registers of baptisms, marriages and burials. PRONI has an almost complete collection of extant Church records, of all denominations, for Northern Ireland.

The quality of the records themselves will vary from denomination to denomination and in some cases from church to church. In order to identify which records exist in a particular area and for what dates researchers should consult the *Guide to Church Records*. This guide lists, alphabetically, churches of all the main denominations that have records deposited at PRONI, and is available on the Search Room shelves. The Public Record Office does not hold records for all churches in Ulster and in some cases these may still be in local custody.

Church of Ireland records

Until 1871 the Church of Ireland was the state church in Ireland. In Belfast it had important civic responsibilities. The parish vestry was used to collect the rates for lighting, paving and watching the town until the middle of the nineteenth century. As a result, the records of the Church of Ireland generally start much earlier than those of the Roman Catholic Church.

The Irish Baptists, Congregationalists, Huguenots, Methodists, Presbyterians and Quakers were all classed by the Church of Ireland and the government as Dissenters. For this reason, in all cases of genealogical research, the parish registers of the Church of Ireland should be examined in any known area of interest, on the chance that the records of a Dissenter from the Church or his earlier family records may be found. This also holds true when searching for information about a person known to have been a Roman Catholic as, in some cases, individuals found it expedient to become converts temporarily, or their families had found it necessary to do so in a previous generation.

Church of Ireland baptismal records usually supply the following information:

- Child's name;
- Father's name;
- Mother's Christian name;
- Name of the officiating clergyman.

It is important to note that the majority of Church of Ireland clergymen recorded burials as well as baptisms and marriages, unlike their Catholic counterparts. These burial registers include the name, age and townland of the deceased and often feature local families of different denominations.

The Church of Ireland also had an important role to play in local administrative as well as religious matters. The concept of an Established Church meant that every person in the parish was considered to be a parishioner regardless of denomination even though he or she did not worship at the local parish church. The vestry meeting held annually on Easter Tuesday was therefore a meeting of all the inhabitants of the parish.

The vestry was an assembly of parishioners who met for the dispatch of parochial business and took its name from its meeting place – the vestry or room in the church in which the priest's vestments were kept. The select vestry was a small committee that could levy taxes for religious purposes – the maintenance of the church and the payment of parish officers such as the sexton and the parish clerk. More important was the general vestry which could raise funds for local services such as poor relief, parish constables, road repair, the organisation of education and the provision of recruits for the Army. In the vestry minute book for the parish of Derriaghy (spelt Dirriaghy), County Antrim, for example, the names are given of members of the Vestry Court, the local constable, the church wardens and those members of the congregation who had contributed money for the benefit of the poor in the area.

Vestry minute books sometimes contain baptism, marriage and burial entries, particularly in the late seventeenth and eighteenth centuries. They often feature items such as the names of the church wardens, of the confirmed, of cess applotters and cess payers, of the poor, the widowed and the orphaned receiving relief, of overseers of the poor and of the roads. The vestry minute books are not only a useful substitute for parishes that have no surviving registers, but they also include details of individuals who were not baptised, married or buried in the parish but who were of some significance locally.

Inevitably vestry records are richest for the cities and large towns; vestry records for rural parishes tend to be less rewarding. Many of the vestry minute books only cover the last 100–150 years. There are, however, exceptions such as the parish of Shankill in Lurgan, the minutes of which go back to 1672 (ref MIC/1E/33) and the vestry minute books for Christ Church Cathedral, Lisburn, which date back to 1675 (MIC/1/4).

Indexes to church registers

A number of indexes are available for church registers. These vary in quality and accuracy but are still worth a look, especially if you have no firm dates as to when an ancestor was married, etc. The following are available on the Search Room shelves at PRONI:

- St George's Church, Belfast – indexed transcription of baptisms and marriages, 1817–70;

- Arboe parish church – index to parish registers, *c.* 1775–1900 (with gaps);

- Kilkeel parish church – index to baptisms, burials and marriages, 1816–42;

- Loughinisland parish church – index to parish registers, 1760–1894;

- Kilskeery parish church – index to parish registers, 1767–1841;

- Killesher parish church – index to parish registers, 1798–1827;

- Killesher parish church – index to parents of children baptised;

- Seagoe parish church – index to parish registers, 1660–1919;

- Donaghadee parish church – index to parish registers, 1771–1845;

- Bangor 1st Presbyterian Church – index to marriages, 1808–45;

- Malone parish church – index to parish registers, 1842–87;

- Lisnaskea parish church – index to baptisms, marriages and burials and publication of banns, 1804–15;

- Lower Badoney parish church – index to parish registers, 1828–37;

- Raphoe parish church – index to marriage licence bonds, 1710–77 and 1817–30.

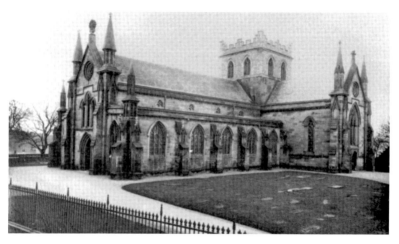

St Patrick's Church of Ireland Cathedral, Armagh, Allison Collection, PRONI A/1/3/3.

Roman Catholic Church records

As a result of the penal laws, which militated against the erection of chapels and regular record-keeping, Roman Catholic registers generally date from a later period than their Protestant counterparts, the majority dating from the 1820s. They are almost entirely for baptisms and marriages, though death or funeral entries do occur occasionally (these generally record only the name of the deceased and the date of death). The baptism entries do, however, include the names of sponsors and the names of witnesses.

Roman Catholic parishes are often made up of parts of more than one civil parish so searching under several parishes is necessary to find all the records of the Roman Catholic parish. Also most Roman Catholic parishes have more than one church. Sometimes only one register was kept for the entire parish, but at other times each church had its own registers.

Catholic baptismal records usually include the following information:

- Date;

- Child's name;

- Father's name;

- Mother's maiden name;

- Names of godparents;

- Parents' residence.

The National Library of Ireland microfilmed almost all the pre-1880 registers in Ireland, but PRONI only had microfilm copies for parishes in Northern Ireland, for most of those in counties Donegal, Cavan and Monaghan, and for some in counties Louth and Leitrim. They are to be found under the reference code MIC/1D. In addition there are some xerox copies under CR/2.

Presbyterian Church records

In general, Presbyterian registers start much later than those of the Church of Ireland, and early records of the Presbyterian baptisms, marriages and deaths are often to be found in the registers of the local Church of Ireland parish. In north-east Ulster, which had a strong Presbyterian population from an early date, some registers date from the late seventeenth and early eighteenth centuries.

A feature of the Presbyterian Church is the number of places that have more than one Presbyterian church and are referred to as 1st, 2nd and 3rd. As well as registers, there are other records of interest to the family and local historian. Instead of vestry minutes, Presyterian churches have session and committee minutes. The former are the most interesting as they sometimes record baptisms and marriages, and the names of new communicants, of those who transgressed and those who left the church, as well as subscription lists. There are often separate communicants' registers which sometimes contain details of deaths, emigrations or transfers to other congregations. A common Presbyterian Church record is the stipend book recording details of those who paid into the church. Seat lists or pew rent books are also common, listing the names of those who had seats rented in the church and occasionally account books and censuses of congregation.

Presbyterian records copied by PRONI are almost exclusively for the nine counties of Ulster and are available under the reference codes MIC/1P and CR/3.

The Presbyterian Historical Society possesses a library of some 12,000 books and pamphlets. The collection includes a large number of congregational histories. Manuscript material includes session minutes, baptisms and marriages from individual churches as well as some presbytery minutes. These include session accounts for Armagh Presbyterian church for 1707–32, session minutes for Aghadowey Presbyterian church for 1702–61 and baptisms from Cullybackey (Cunningham Memorial) Presbyterian church covering the period 1726–1815. The Society also has a duplicate set of the microfilm copies of Presbyterian Church registers held by PRONI covering the vast majority of Presbyterian congregations in Ireland.

Methodist records

John Wesley, the founder of Methodism, first visited Ireland in 1747 and when he died in 1791 the Methodists were well established there with 67 preachers and a membership of over 14,000, most of whom were from Ulster. He spoke at local market houses or session houses and held open-air services. Occasionally sympathetic ministers would allow him to speak at the local meeting house. However, not even the Earl of Moira could persuade the rector in the village to allow Wesley to speak at the church. Such was their interest in Wesley's teachings that, for a time, the Earl and Countess of Moira opened the great hall of their mansion for weekly public services conducted by Methodist preachers.

The majority of its members were, nevertheless, members of the Established Church and they remained members of their own churches. Therefore they continued to go to the parish church for the administration of marriages, burials and baptism until the early nineteenth century when Methodists began to assert their independence. In 1816 a split developed between the Primitive Wesleyan Methodists, who retained their links with the Established Church, and the Wesleyan Methodists, who allowed their ministers to administer baptisms.

As a result the majority of Methodist baptism registers do not begin until the 1830s and the marriages until 1845. There are few Methodist burial registers because Methodist churches simply did not have their own burial grounds. However, an important record is a large volume of baptism entries for Methodist churches throughout Ireland which is among the administrative records of the Methodist Church in Ireland (MIC/429/1) and which may have been the product of an attempt to compile a central register of baptisms. Although incomplete, it contains baptisms from 1815 to 1840 and often pre-dates existing individual church baptism registers (PRONI MIC/1E and CR/6).

The Religious Society of Friends (or Quakers)

The Religious Society of Friends, also known as Quakers or Friends, orginated in the north-west of England during the mid-seventeenth century. The Quaker movement was brought to Ireland by William Edmundson, who was born in 1627 in Westmoreland, England, when he established a business in Dublin in 1652. A few years later he moved north to Lurgan, County Armagh and by the mid-seventeenth century, settlements were firmly established in Lurgan and around Lisburn, County Antrim. According to Edmundson's journal for the year 1655, the movement found the citizens of Belfast largely unreceptive:

> At this time but few would lodge us in their houses; at Belfast (that town of great profession) there was but one of all the Inns and Public Houses that would lodge any of our friends, which was one Widow Partridge, who kept a Public House, and received us very kindly; there John Tiffin lodged, often endeavouring to get an entrance for truth in that town, but they resisted, shutting their Ears, Doors, and Hearts against it.

Near the end of the eighteenth century, one or two Quaker families settled at Belfast. This small congregation held its meetings in a back store belonging to one of the members. By 1812, the increase in numbers persuaded the growing congregation to take a plot of ground in Frederick Street, where they built a small meeting house.

From the beginning there was a strong emphasis on record-keeping. This included registers of births (not baptisms, as baptism was not practised by the Society of Friends), marriages and burials. Minute books record in great detail the work, organisation and oversight of meetings, including details about sufferings and records of births, marriages and deaths (sometimes arranged by family name).

PRONI has copied all the records at the Lisburn Meeting House which include not only those of Lisburn, but of Lurgan, Ballyhagen and Richhill in County Armagh, Grange near Charlemont, County Tyrone and Antrim and Cootehill, County Monaghan. They are to be found under the reference code MIC/16 and CR/8.

Congregational Church records

Congregationalists came to Ireland in the seventeenth century but made little impact until the early nineteenth century. The setting up of the Irish

Evangelical Society in 1814 resulted in many churches being built. PRONI holds some records of the Congregational churches in Dublin and of the church at Carrickfergus (which has baptisms from 1819 to the present). The only records copied are those of Straid. All of these will be found under the reference code CR/7.

Baptist Church records

Although the Baptists were among the independent churches that came into Ireland in the mid-seventeenth century, it was the nineteenth century before they began to make progress in Ulster. The movement was confined largely to Ulster and recruits were drawn predominately from small farming or industrial working-class backgrounds. The earliest records in PRONI's custody begin in the 1860s and consist of marriages and minute books. As the Baptist Church does not practise infant baptism, there are no baptism registers, but details of those who came into membership can be found in the minute books. They do not have any burial grounds hence the absence of burial registers. PRONI has some Baptist Church records, but you will find many more in the custody of the churches or with the Baptist Union of Belfast.

Non-Subscribing Presbyterian Church (or Unitarians)

The Non-Subscribing Presbyterian Church has its origins as far back as 1725 when a number of congregations refused to subscribe to the Westminster Confession of Faith and formed themselves into a separate Presbytery of Antrim. Some of the early Non-Subscribing Presbyterian Church records, created before the split, are in fact Presyterian records: for example, the early records of Scarva Street Presbyterian Church in Banbridge are to be found in Banbridge Non-Subscribing Presbyterian Church records.

Church records also contain a wide variety of material that is of interest to genealogists. These include communicant's rolls, lists of subscribers, pew rent books, ordinations lists and censuses taken by local ministers. An example of the latter can be found in the records of Rademon, Non-Subscribing Presbyterian Church, County Down. A census was taken, 1835–36, and is more than just a list of names. Included are comments such as 'All left the country except the wife who is a wretched beggar'; 'All away gone to bad'; 'Turned out of their farm by the Landlord and left without a home – Emigrated to New South Wales'.

PRONI has copied some Non-Subscribing Presbyterian Church records and some have also been deposited. The records can be found under the reference code MIC/1B or CR/4.

Reformed Presbyterian Church (or Covenanters)

The Reformed Presbyterian Church had its origins in the seventeenth century, when a minority of Presbyterians wished to adhere

Monastery of Glenarm, The Scenery and Antiquities of Ireland, *drawn by W H Bartlett (1841).*

more strictly to the Covenants of 1638 and 1642. However, it was not until the mid-eighteenth century that congregations were formed with their own ordained ministers. The earliest records begin mainly in the mid-nineteenth century, apart from some early nineteenth-century sessions minuted for Cullybackey, County Antrim and Drumolg, County Londonderry. Some have been copied by PRONI and can be found under the reference codes MIC/1C and CR/5.

Moravian Church records

The Moravian Church was founded in the eighteenth century in what is now the Czech Republic, arriving in Ireland in 1746 when the first Moravian Church was founded in Dublin. Within two years there were societies in most Ulster counties. From these sprang the congregations making up the Moravian Church in Ireland – Ballinderry, Kilwarlin, Cracehill, Cracefield, Belfast (University Road and Cliftonville) and Dublin.

Apart from baptism, marriage and burial registers, the Moravian Church also maintains very detailed membership registers recording for each member date of birth, previous denomination, when deceased or left and the reason for leaving. Ministers' diaries contain births, marriages and deaths, the names of those who joined the Church and those who left and lists of members.

PRONI has copied all the records held at Gracehill Moravian church, which comprise not only those for Gracehill but also for other churches including the Dublin church. All these records can be found under the reference code MIC/1F and CR/7.

Huguenot records

Savage religious persecution in their native France drove French Calvinists, known as Huguenots, from their country in large numbers. Some 10,000 made their way to Ireland where they were welcomed by the Ascendancy for their Protestantism and for their industry and because they strengthened the Protestant community. An Act of 1692 'for encouragement of protestant strangers' specifically allowed such strangers (who did not include Scots) to worship 'in their own several rites used in their own countries'.

The most important Huguenot settlement in Ulster was founded in Lisburn (originally called Lisnagarvey). William III's bill to foster the linen trade in 1697 resulted in more than seventy French families, led by Louis Crommelin, to establish the industry in Lisburn. Some refugees who arrived in Lisburn before 1704 attended the Church of Ireland in Lambeg or Lisburn cathedal. Both registers contain many Huguenot names. The actual Huguenot registers were lost in the mid-nineteenth century and all subsequent efforts to trace them have failed. Many Huguenot names appear in the local Church of Ireland registers. For example, the burial entries for Christ Church Cathedal, Lisburn, show a large number of military funerals in 1689 when the Duke of Schomberg quartered his troops in Lisburn.

The Huguenot Society of Great Britain and Ireland was established in 1885 to collect and publish information relating to the history and genealogy of Huguenots. The Huguenot Library, at University College, Gower Street, London WC1, contains much material on Irish Huguenot families not available elsewhere, including manuscripts, pedigrees and collections of family papers. An Irish Section of the Society was established in 1987. All members of the Society receive a copy of *Huguenot Proceedings*, a useful work of reference for the family historian. An Annual General Meeting is convened in Ireland each year and a church service, in St Patrick's Cathedral, Dublin, is held each November.

Jewish records

A small but vibrant Jewish community has also settled in Belfast over the centuries. A synagogue on the Somerton Road still ministers to the local Jewish community. Distinguished members of the community include Chaim Herzog, President of Israel from 1983–93, and the current Chancellor of the University of Ulster, Rabbi Julia Neuberger.

Of particular interest are transcripts of tombstone inscriptions from the Jewish cemetery in the city, *c.* 1874–1954, PRONI, T/1602, from which the following extract is taken:

	Date of Death	*Date of Birth*
Herman Boas	12 Jan 1917	30 Apr 1827
Caroline Boas	13 Nov 1916	8 May 1839
Edward Boas	6 June 1918	8 Jan 1875
Sarah Bernstein	17 Oct 1917	
Louis Bernstein	3 May 1909	6 Jan 1876
Samuel Bernstein	2 May 1904	24 July 1874
George Betzold	10 Feb 1890	22 Apr 1834
Florence Betzold	5 Sep 1880	13 Aug 1880
Maurice Librach	20 Jan 1952	
Anne Librach	15 July 1940	
Felix Harold Librach	29 Oct 1917	2 Jan 1900

It is also worth consulting *The Jews in Ireland from the Earliest Times to the Year 1910* (London, 1972) by R Hyman.

Census returns

It is worth checking the church records of a particular area for census returns compiled by the local clergy. These can vary in scale from a list of a specific congregation or of the whole parish. The so-called 'visiting book' for Sallaghy parish, County Fermangh, for example, was really a census for the year 1847 arranged alphabetically under townlands and giving the age of each member of the family, including Roman Catholic families, acreage and rents of farms. There is a similar 'visiting book' for Galloon parish, including Newtownbutler, County Fermanagh for the years 1847–48. D/2098.

The following are just a few of the census records compiled by local clergy:

- Census of the congregation, *c.* 1850, Magilligan, County Londonderry, MIC/1P/215;

- Census of the congregation, 1836–37, Rademon, County Down, CR/4/2;

- Census of the parish of Clondevaddock, 1796, County Donegal, MIC/1/164;

- Census, 1846, Ballycastle Presbyterian church, MIC/1P/115;

- Census of the parish of Mount Charles, 1867–68, County Donegal, MIC/1/158;

- Volume containing census returns for the united parishes of Rathaspick and Russagh, County Westmeath, compiled by the Revd H W Stewart, with references to those who emigrated to the USA and Australia, 1863–72, T/2786;

Devenish Island, The Scenery and Antiquities of Ireland, *drawn by W H Bartlett (1841).*

- Census of the congregation, 1843, and lists of emigrants, 1854–84, for Cortin, County Tyrone, MIC/1P/253;

- Census of the parish of Glenavy, County Antrim, 1856–57, and revisions, 1858–59 and 1873, CR/1/53;

- Censuses, 1821–39, Ballyblack, County Down, MIC/1P/318;

- Book containing a list of the inhabitants of the parish of Termot [Termonmaguirk, County Tyrone?], *c.* 1780, DIO/4/32/T/4;

- Register of families, 1st Ballymoney congregation, 1817, CR/3/10/1.

Marriage licence bonds

Marriage licence bonds were issued by the bishops of the dioceses of the Established Church. The original bonds were destroyed in 1922, but there are indexes to these bonds and these indexes are available. They contain the names of the bridegroom and bride and the date of the bond.

Indexes to marriage licence bonds at PRONI:

- Prerogative Court, Dublin, *c.* 1625 to 1857

T/932/1.   A to D (in date order by letters);
2.   E to Z (in date order by letters);
3.   A to Z (in red ink, man's name before wife's);
            A to M (in black ink, names mixed);
4.   S to Y (in red ink, wife's maiden name before husband's name);
            M to TUK (in black ink, names mixed);

5.   TUL to Y (in black ink, names mixed);
        P to S (in red ink, wife's maiden name before husband's name);
        A to P (in black ink, wife's maiden name before husband's name).

Note: Only volumes 1 and 2 need normally be used.

•   Prerogative Court, Dublin, *c*. 1595 to 1857
Grants of probate, Intestacy and Marriage Licenses

MIC/ 7/8.   A 1811 to E 1830;
  9.   F 1821 to G 1844;
  10.   G 1844 to Y 1857;
  11.   M to Z 1811 to 1857;
  12A.   A to B 1692 to 1697;
            A to E 1595 to 1810;
  12B.   F to R 1595 to 1810;
  12C.   R to Z 1595 to 1810.

•   Diocese of Armagh

MIC/5B/1.   A to Greenaway, part 1, 1727 to 1845;
    2.   A to Greenaway, part 2, 1727 to 1845;
            Greenaway – Miller 1727 to 1845;
    3.   Miller – Young 1727 to 1845.

•   Diocese of Dromore

MIC/5B/4.   1709 to 1861 plus index 1630 to 1800.

•   Diocese of Down, Connor and Dromore

MIC/5B/5.   1721 to 1845 part 1;
    6.   1721 to 1845 part 2.

Chapter 8

SCHOOL RECORDS

In the early years of the nineteenth century the education system in Ireland was in a chaotic and disorganised state. There were some charter schools which were established by royal charter in 1733 for the education of the poor receiving grants from the Irish Parliament, and built by private subscription. Many landlords also took an interest in education. Lord Lurgan, for example, established Lurgan Free School on his estate in 1783 which provided education for the children of tenants regardless of religion. Mr and Mrs Hall, who toured Ireland shortly before the Great Famine, commented:

> The principal proprietor of Tandragee is Lord Manderville, who, with his neighbours, Lords Farnham and Roden, Colonel Blacker and the Marquis of Downshire, have contributed largely to the present cheering condition of the County of Armagh. Lord Manderville has established no fewer than sixteen district schools on his estate in this neighbourhood, for the support of which he devotes £1,000 per annum, out of an income which is by no means large.

Statutory provision for a system of education in Ireland had been in existence since the sixteenth century. In 1537 Henry VIII aimed to end 'the certain savage and wild kind and manner of living' of the Irish by providing for the establishment of elementary schools in each parish, the prime purpose of which was the teaching of the English language. Nevertheless, the task of organising and maintaining the parish schools had been assigned to the Anglican clergy who, being usually poor and non-resident, found it impossible to overcome local hostility. Bishop Nicholson of Carlisle, who later became Bishop of Derry, complained in 1714 that the poor in Ireland still spoke Irish and that they were not sending their children to the parish schools mainly because the schoolmaster expected payment which they were unable to make.

Lurgan Model School, Lawrence Collection, PRONI.

While the penal laws were enforced, Irish peasants had no alternative but to depend upon hedge schools for their elementary education. These were basically a collection of ragged students and a teacher holding class in a ditch or hedgerow, with one of the pupils serving as a look-out for law officers. These were usually set up by itinerant schoolmasters who were paid according to the size of the school. They first appeared towards the end of the seventeenth century when wandering scholars found it necessary to hide themselves in remote places away from official view. Arthur Young, who travelled through Ireland in the 1770s, wrote of encountering 'many a ditch full of travellers'. As the penal laws were relaxed the master was able to make himself and his pupils a bit more comfortable, settling in the comparative luxury of a sod hut or an unused barn for his classroom.

An alternative to hedge schools or those founded by religious orders was provided by various Protestant societies for the conversion of Roman Catholics. The Irish charity school movement began in the early eighteenth century under voluntary auspices. In most cases the charity schools enrolled both Protestant and Catholic children, but permitted instruction only in the Protestant faith. In 1717 the Society in Dublin for Promoting Christian Knowledge was formed under the leadership of Dr Henry Maule, later Protestant Bishop of Meath and by 1725 the Society was operating 163 schools with 3,000 pupils.

A similar society, known as the 'charter school society', was able to obtain a royal charter. So-called from the charter of George III (6 February 1734) by which the Incorporated Society in Dublin for Promoting English Protestant Schools in Ireland was established. It was specified that 'the children of the Popish and other poor natives' were to be instructed in the English tongue and the formularies of the Established Church of

Ireland. It aimed to provide a means of educating the children of Catholics 'before the corruptions of popery have taken root in their hearts', and to produce Protestant wives for English settlers who in the past had married Catholics because they had no choice. It was considered essential that the schools be boarding schools so that the children would be removed from the influence of their parents and priests. For this reason the schools were located in the more remote parts of the country.

The Society for the Education of the Poor in Ireland, better known as the Kildare Place Society, was founded in 1811 and aimed to provide a system of interdenominational education. For a time it had the approval of the Catholic clergy and laymen. Daniel O'Connell was on the Society's board of governors, Catholic clergy became patrons of individual schools and the clergy gave their cautious sanction to the Society's activities. In 1820, however, the Kildare Place Society abandoned its neutral stance and began to allocate part of its own income to the schools of various Protestant proselytising societies, such as the London Hibernian Society, the Baptist Society and the Association for Discountenancing Vice. O'Connell resigned in 1820 and led an agitation against the Society. A petition signed by the leading Catholic bishops led in 1824 to the establishment of another official inquiry into Irish popular education. By 1830 the number of schools had risen to 1,634, but that same year the Parliament grant was withdrawn and the number of schools quickly declined.

In the early years of the nineteenth century although there were numerous schools in Northern Ireland (Counties Antrim and Down had over 1,000 schools between them), they were fragmented in structure and were largely boycotted by Roman Catholics. It was against this background of haphazard education and falling standards of living that the Irish system of National Education was founded in 1831 under the direction of the Chief Secretary, E G Stanley. The national schools that resulted were built with the aid of the Commissioners of National Education and local trustees. The curriculum was to be secular in content, though provision was made for separate religious instruction at special stated times. The Board gave assistance to local committees in building schools and made a major contribution towards the teacher's salaries. A teacher-training school was established in Dublin. Model schools were gradually set up throughout the county.

The main criticism of the new system came from the churches. The Established Church was suspicious of these attempts to remove their influence over the education system. Ironically, the Roman Catholic clergy remained wary of what they continued to see as a proselytising organisation. Mr and Mrs Hall, who remembered the old school houses as 'for the

most part, wretched hovels, in which the boys and girls mixed indiscrimi-
nately', were impressed by the transformation brought about by the Board
of Education: 'The school-houses, instead of being dark, close, dirty and
unwholesome, are neat and commodius buildings, well-ventilated and in
all respects healthful'. They were also impressed with the books supplied
by the Board. These included an 'English Grammar, Arithmetic books for
various classes; books geometry, book keeping; An Introduction to the Art
of Reading and a Treatise on Mensuration'.

As well as receiving an education, girls were taught needlework and the
National Education Board encouraged the teaching of agriculture and
gardening to boys and girls. The priorities of the Commissioners of
National Education were set out in a set of instructions given to inspectors
in 1836: 'He [the inspector] will ascertain the advancement of education
among the children, noting the proportion of children who can read
fluently; what progress they have made in writing and arithmetic; whether
any be taught geography, grammar, book-keeping and mensuration;
whether girls be taught sewing or knitting'.

It is worth pointing out that although by the end of the nineteenth
century free elementary schooling was provided for all children, the
numbers attending schools in many areas was sparse. John McEvoy, in his
A Statistical Survey of County Tyrone, published in 1802, commented that:

With respect to education, attainable from day-schools by the lower
class, very little real benefit can be derived; as, when children are able
to perform any sort of work, such as herding of cattle, they are then
taken from school. From the age of six or seven, to that of ten or
eleven years, is the usual time for children to be kept at school; as this
early period they acquire but little, and that little is generally
forgotten, before they come to the age of understanding.

Although Acts of 1876 and 1880 prohibited the employment of children
under 10 years and children up to 13 were required to attend school, the
reports of the Commission for Education make it clear that many children
only attended school infrequently. In his general report into the Armagh
Circuit of 1903, Mr Murphy commented that:

The character of the attendance remains practically unchanged. The
same causes are at work in town and in country and the same unsat-
isfactory results are noticeable. In rural districts the pupils attend for
the most part very irregularly. This is due to the demand for child
labour, and partly to a seeming inability on the part of parents to

appreciate the injustice they do to their children, when they keep them from school without sufficient reason.

For much of the nineteenth century there was no state system of secondary education and what was available was provided by a small number of voluntary schools. When the national system of education was introduced in 1831 many schools that had provided intermediate education ceased to do so because the new Board of Education would only support primary education. In 1837 the Wyse Committee recommended the provision of a centrally funded non-denominational system of intermediate education but until the passage of the 1878 Intermediate Education Act, second-level education was available only in the Protestant diocesan, Royal and Erasmus Smith schools.

As early as 1608, James I decreed that at least one free grammar school should be established in each of the six confiscated Ulster counties. The objectives were: 'To stir up and recall the province of Ulster from superstition, rebellion, calamity and poverty to the true religion of Christ, and to obedience, strength and prosperity'. By 1625 royal free schools had been established at Dungannon, County Tyrone, Enniskillen, County Fermanagh and Cavan, Armagh and Raphoe, County Donegal. Enniskillen was one the royal schools founded on a grant of land by James I in 1617. The school stands in a magnificent setting just outside the town of Enniskillen. Oscar Wilde was sent to Portora in February 1864; he was 10 and younger than most of the entrants at that time. Wilde threw himself into the school activities and became a popular character. He later told a friend:

I was looked upon as a prodigy by my associates because, quite frequently, I would, for a wager, read a three-volume novel in half an hour so closely as to be able to give an accurate resume of the plot of the story; by one hour's reading I was enabled to give a fair narrative of the incidental scenes and the most pertinent dialogue.

Despite their limitations, school records are an invaluable source for family historians. At their best they can help to make up for the loss of the nineteenth-century census records. If you do not know the school that your ancestor attended, the first step is to find the location of school in the area where he or she lived. This can be done using commercial street directories that list schools from the middle of the nineteenth century. Ordnance Survey maps and the Ordnance Survey Memoirs may also provide useful information.

Allstragh School,
c. 1901, PRONI,
Allison Collection,
A/2/3/1.

PRONI has in its custody material that pre-dates the introduction of the national school system in the 1830s and a number of these items contain records that are of interest to family historians. These records include the minute books of the Southwell Charity School, Downpatrick, County Down, 1722–1970 (ref D/2961), the records of Lurgan Free School, established for the education of poor children in Shankill parish (ref D/1928/S) and records of Watts Endowed School, later re-named Lurgan College (D/2664). For a more complete list see the *Guide to Educational Records*, which is available on the shelves of the Public Search Room.

Between 1832 and 1870 something in the region of 2,500 national schools were established in Ulster and the records that have survived for schools in Antrim, Armagh, Down, Fermanagh, Londonderry and Tyrone are held in PRONI. Of particular interest to genealogists are the registers of about 1,500 national and public elementary schools. These registers generally date from the 1860s and they record the full name of the pupil, date of birth (or age of entry), religion, father's address and occupation, details of attendance and academic progress and the name of the school previously attended. A space is also provided in the registers for general comments which might tell you where the children went to work afterwards or if he/she emigrated. Some have an index at the front that can greatly ease searching. In many ways the information contained in the registers for this period can compensate for the lack of census records in the nineteenth century.

PRONI's *Guide to Educational Records* includes an alphabetical list of all the schools for which it holds records. Further information on using the school register collection at PRONI will be found in an article by Trevor Parkhill, 'School Records and their Value for Genealogical Research', in *Familia, Ulster Genealogical Review*, no. 1 (1985), 81–85.

Secondary education

The need for secondary education increased with the demands of the growing middle class in Belfast. Colleges were created to meet the needs of the various religious communities in Belfast. The Methodist College was opened in 1868; Campbell College – a Presbyterian school run on the lines of an English boarding school – was opened in 1864; St Malacy's College, established in 1833 and rebuilt in 1867, was the first Catholic secondary school for boys as well as a diocesan seminary; and St Dominic's High School for girls, opened on the Falls Road in 1870.

The Methodist College was opened in 1868. It was established to give theological training to young men intended for the Wesleyan ministry. There was also a boarding and day seminary which aimed to prepare students for careers in business or for entrance to Queen's University. *The Register of Methodist College, 1868–1984* has been compiled by Paul Fry and a copy is available at the Linen Hall Library.

Campbell College, Belmont, was opened in 1894 in accordance with the will of the late H J Campbell, who left about £200,000 to build a high-class public school. Campbell College registers have been published in 1913, 1927, 1938 and 1954. The most recent volume was published in 1982 and contains details of pupils from 1894–1982 and is available at the Linen Hall Library and Central Library.

Presbyterians were interested in the education of candidates for the ministry and took a leading part in the founding of the Belfast Academy in 1785. However, the Academy did not provide courses of a university character, forcing students to continue their education at Scottish universities. The Academy began life on the edge of town in what is still called Academy Street. This institution succeeded in running a little medical school and other departments for higher education for some years and the Academy settled down to a career as a simple boys' school. In 1880 the Academy moved to new premises on the Cliftonville Road. In 1901 it began to admit girls to a special department and in 1924 the school became completely co-educational. PRONI also holds the records of Belfast Academy in the form of minutes and accounts (D/1905/2).

It was not until after the establishment of the Academical Institution in 1810 that Ulster Presbyterian ministers could receive their training at home. In the course of time the Academical Institution also became a boys' school under the affectionate name of 'Inst'. PRONI holds the records of the Royal Belfast Academical Institution and these contain names of pupils names dating back to 1810 (SCH/524). There are five volumes of 'albums', 1814–1918, which are registers of pupils of the collegiate part of the school giving, as well as names, details of examinations sat and some information on subsequent careers. Records of the Royal Belfast Academical Institution are held by PRONI, reference SCH/524.

Third-level education

The Academical Institution's function as a college of higher education was taken over when the Queen's College, founded in 1845, was opened in 1849. Trinity College, Dublin, the only university in Ireland, excluded Catholics and Dissenters from degrees and appointments. In 1845 Robert Peel's government decided to establish the Queen's Colleges in Belfast, Cork and Galway. Though officially non-denominational, the College inevitably reflected the predominance of Presbyterians among its supporters and students. Queen's College acquired university status under the Irish Universities Act 1908.

Child's Name	Parent's Name	Denomination	Residence	Age	Progress
James Lynes	William & Jane	Papists	BallyBlough	9	Spelling mono syl
David Smart	Archibald & Elizbth	Presbyter	Lurgan	8	Spelling mono syl
Ralph Smart	DoDo	DoDo		6	Beginning Letters
John McCarten	Dennis & Mary	Papists	Do	13	Spelling mono syl
John Morgan	John & —	Do	Stonewall		Beginning Letters
Robert McMahon	John & Margaret	Church	BallyBlough	12	Spelling mono syl
Thos Bullock	Charles & Ann	Do	Back Lane	6	Beginning Letters

Researchers interested in ancestors who may have gone to Queen's College/University should consult the annual *University Calendars* which list students for each academic year for the period 1850–1920. Annual lists were not produced after 1920 because the increasing number of graduates made it impractical. The *University Calendars* are held by the main library at Queen's.

The extract on the previous page, dating from 11 September 1786, illustrates the quality of these records.

Chapter 9

VALUATION AND TITHE RECORDS

Tithe applotment books, 1823–38

The tithe was not a tax but a charge upon land. The tithe system, which nominally earmarked one-tenth of the produce of the land for the mainte- nance of the clergy, was introduced in England as early as the eighth century. It was introduced to Ireland during the reign of Henry II, although it was not paid outside the area around Dublin until the reign of Elizabeth I.

In many parishes in Ulster a tithe composition or modus had become customary by which parishioners were able to pay a fixed sum of money for each form of tithe. In 1775 for the parish of Shankill in north Armagh tithes levied included: 1s from every tradesman, 2s and 6d from every shopkeeper and 1d from every owner of a garden, at Easter; 9d for each new milch cow calving within the previous year, and 4½d for every stripper cow.

Sadly very few of the eighteenth-century title records have survived. In 1823 the Tithe Applotment Act was passed, which stipulated that hence- forth all tithes due to the Established Church were to be paid in money rather than in kind, as they previously could have been. Between 1823 and 1827 holdings in each civil parish were valued based on the average price of wheat and oats in the parish during the seven years preceding 1 November 1821. This necessitated a complete valuation of all tithable land in Ireland, the results of which are contained in the manuscript tithe- applotment books for each civil parish.

The tithe-applotment books are unique records giving details of land occupation and valuations for individual holdings prior to the devastation brought about by the Great Famine and the resulting mass emigration.

Giant's Causeway, The Scenery and Antiquities of Ireland, *drawn by W H Bartlett (1841).*

They list the occupiers of tithable land and are not a list of householders, as is the case in a census. Therefore, landless labourers and weavers were omitted, in addition to all purely urban dwellers.

In 1838 the tithe payment was reduced by 25 per cent and transferred from the tenant to the landowner. Tithes were finally abolished in Ireland in 1869. The names of the tithe payers are usually arranged alphabetically by townlands and by parish and county. Unfortunately there are no accompanying maps to show land division on a field-by-field basis.

More than 270 volumes are held by PRONI for parishes in Counties Antrim, Armagh, Cavan, Down, Fermanagh, Londonderry and Tyrone, reference Number FIN/5A. Indexes to townlands and personal names in the tithe-applotment books are available on microfilm (MIC/15K).

Copies of tithe-applotment books can also be found in the records of the Episcopalian Church and in some estate collections. Unfortunately there are no maps relating to these tithe-applotment records.

A CD-ROM index to the tithe-applotment books for counties Antrim, Armagh, Derry, Down, Fermanagh and Tyrone is available as *Tithe Applotment Books, 1823–1838*, while a CD-ROM index to the *Primary Valuation* is available as *Index to Griffith's Valuation of Ireland, 1848–1864* (both from Genealogical Publishing Co. Ltd, Baltimore, USA).

Valuation records

PRONI holds records relating to the valuation of property in the area covered by Northern Ireland from the 1830s to 1975. A series of valuations were taken in that time: 1830s, 1860s, 1864–1929, 1935, 1956 and 1975. The original purpose was, and remains, the assessment of every building and every piece of land and estimating its financial value. The valuation is, in theory, the amount the owner would expect to receive if he hired out his property for one year. The valuation of a property is subsequently used in assessing the rates to be paid.

The levying of a rate in Ireland, to raise money to meet the costs of local government, dates from 1635. An Act of that year give Justices of the Peace power to levy certain sums, known as the County Cess or Grand Jury Cess, upon the inhabitants of a local area for the execution of public works such as roads and bridges. By 1824, Parliament recognised the need for a more equitable method of measuring liability for cess and rates. The 1st Valuation Act was introduced in 1826 and a valuation of the whole of Ireland was prepared.

Though often dismissed as being of fairly limited genealogical value, the townland valuation carried out in the 1830s can be an important source for those searching for their ancestors, particularly if those ancestors were urban dwellers. The records consist of manuscript field books (more than 4,500) compiled by parish, which described each townland in the parish, the quality of the aril and its valuations. Although the townland valuation was primarily concerned with the agricultural value of land, it also included details on houses valued at £3 or over (in 1838 this was raised to £5 or over but by this time most of Ulster had been surveyed). In the rural areas the names of only a few householders were given, and these tended to be of the gentry or the better class of tenant farmers. In towns, however, many more houses were substantial enough to reach the valuation, with the result that a large number of householders are recorded.

Unfortunately, major towns and villages are not listed separately, but under the heading of the parish and barony in which they are located. Those for Northern Ireland are available at PRONI under the reference VAL/1B; the accompanying annotated maps are listed under VAL/1A and VAL/1D.

In order to locate the appropriate volume for the major towns and villages it is necessary to find out which parish they are listed under. This can be done by consulting the *Alphabetical Index to the Townlands and Towns, Parishes and Baronies of Ireland*, which is available on the shelves of the Public Search Room at PRONI and the NAI. It is simply a matter of locating the relevant town and then running a finger along the columns listing the barony, parish and Poor Law Union.

The first general valuation (Griffith), 1848–64

By contrast, the 1848–64 valuation gives a complete list of occupiers of land, tenements and houses. This *Primary Valuation* of Ireland, better known as Griffith's, was to determine the amount of tax, or rates, each person should pay towards the support of the poor and destitute within each Poor Law Union. The value of all privately held lands and buildings in both rural and urban areas was determined according to the rate at which each property could be rented year after year. The tax was fixed at about 6 per cent (with variations) for every pound of the rent value, and was arranged by county, within counties by Poor Law Union division, and within Unions by parish. It included the following information:

- Name of the townland;

- Name of the householder or leaseholder;

- Name of the person from whom the property was leased;

- Description of the property;

- Acreage;

- Valuation of the land and buildings.

Hillmount Bleachgreen, County Antrim, Ulster Museum.

The published version of *Griffith's Valuation* was based on the valuers' notebooks. It did not, however, include all the information provided by the notebook, and some entries in the later published version have been updated. Earlier surveys were not included. PRONI has, for example, fifty-nine manuscript volumes containing the Valuation of Antrim, 1939, Cavan, 1841 and Down, 1839. A valuation of the city of Armagh was published in 1839. It contains the name and annual value of every holding in the city. A copy is available at the Irish Studies Library, Armagh and the NLI. County and city libraries will normally hold these volumes relating to their localities.

Griffith's Valuation is of particular interest to anyone wishing to trace their family tree, due to the fact that so little of the nineteenth-century census returns has survived. It is especially important for identifying emigrants to their precise place of origin during this period. Emigration statistics point to the fact that a large proportion of the mass emigration that took place as a result of the Great Famine of 1845–51 did not occur until after 1855, by which time the valuation was largely complete for the south and west of the county.

Family historians should be aware that *Griffith's Valuation* has some limitations. Partnership farms held under the rundale system had their individual parcels bracketed together without been separately measured, thereby excluding certain tenant names.

The original notebooks for Northern Ireland are available at PRONI, reference VAL/2B. The valuer's annotated set of Ordnance Survey maps showing the location of every property is available at PRONI (VAL/2A).

Printed editions of *Griffith's Valuation* are available in the Public Search Rooms of the NAI and PRONI and at major libraries throughout Ireland. These volumes are arranged by Poor Law Union, within union by county, and then into parishes and townlands. There is an index at the front of each volume which enables searchers to identify the page or pages in which a specific townland may be found.

An index to *Griffith's Valuation* for all of Ireland is available on CD-ROM from Heritage World in Donaghmore. A CD-ROM set comprising page scans of the printed *Griffith's Valuation* has also been produced by Irish Microfilms Media Ltd in Dublin.

Valuation revisions

Another set of useful records are the 'Cancelled Land Books' and 'Current Land Books' which give details of all changes in the holdings, from the time of *Griffith's Valuation* to the present day. When a change of occupancy occurred, the name of the lessee or householder was crossed off and the new owner's name written above it, while the year was noted on the right-hand side of the page. This helps to establish significant dates in family history, such as dates of death, sale or emigration. By the closing years of the nineteenth century most of the occupiers of land had become landowners, thanks to a series of land-purchase acts. This explains the initials LAP (Land Act Purchase) that may be found stamped on an entry in the revision lists. These volumes are arranged by Poor Law Union within counties, and then into parishes and townlands. There is an index at the front of each volume which enables searchers to identify the page or pages in which a specific townland may be found. The *Householders' Index* can be used as a guide to the surnames listed in *Griffith's Valuation*.

PRONI holds those for Northern Ireland, reference VAL/12B. The corresponding maps are also available, reference VAL/12D.

Revaluation of Belfast, 1900–6

Belfast was the only council to exercise the revaluation option granted to local councils by the Local Govenment (Ireland) Act 1898. The valuators' notebooks, in which the appeals against valuation and the re-valuation were recorded, are to be found in VAL/7B. These valuation books are arranged by ward and there is an index in the catalogue that not only gives the reader the names of the streets to be found in each volume but also the numbers of the pages on which the street is recorded.

This revaluation, carried out at a time when Belfast was reckoned to be the fastest growing city in the British Isles, is a particularly valuable source for any family historian wishing to trace ancestors who migrated to the city at this time.

First Northern Ireland General Revaluation, 1935–54

The First General Revaluation came into force on 1 April 1936. As a result of the Second World War the Second Revaluation did not take effect until 1 April 1957 so that the earlier revaluation, the first undertaken after the establishment of the Government of Northern Ireland, is an important source for family historians interested in the more recent past. The valuation books contain the names of both the occupier of a particular property and the name of the immediate lessor (VAL/3B). The revision lists are also available and these detail changes in the ownership of property, etc. until the mid-1950s (VAL/3D).

The maps that accompany this valuation are available, on the scale 6in to mile, reference VAL/3A.

Chapter 10

LANDED ESTATE RECORDS

Ulster, like the rest of Ireland, was a predominantly rural society until the middle of the nineteenth century. At the same time Ulster, until well into the nineteenth century, reflected its colonial beginnings remaining as it did a province of large estates. By the middle of the century more than three-quarters of the Irish population lived in rural areas working in agriculture or in agricultural-related occupations. The Irish countryside was made up of great estates where, by the 1870s, more than half the land was owned by less than 1,000 major landlords, many of them related by blood or marriage. Many proprietors, like the Dukes of Devonshire, lived most of the year in England, returning occasionally to their Irish estates, which were partly sub-let to lesser landlords and partly managed in their absence by agents or middlemen. At the other end of the social scale were the poor labourers walking the roads in search of work. In their absence their families frequently lived by begging, especially during the 'hungry months' or 'meal months' of June and July after the year's stock of potatoes had been used up and before the new ones became available.

The major landowners managed great estates that were often distributed through two or three counties; the Marquis of Downshire had 115,000 acres in Antrim, Down, Kildare, King's County and Wicklow; Lord Landsdowne owned 120,000 acres in Counties Dublin, Kerry, Limerick, Meath and Queen's; and the Marquess of Conyngham owned more than 156,000 acres in Clare, Donegal and Meath. Visitors to Ireland were struck by the great mansion houses like Powerscourt, Castletown and Castle Coole. Traditionally referred to as 'big houses' by the local community, in most cases the size of the landed estate dictated the size of the big house. Chevalier de la Tocnaye, a Frenchman who travelled through Ireland in the 1790s, was impressed by Lord Belmore's classical house, Castle Coole, in County Fermanagh:

Lord Belmore has just built in this neighbourhood, a superb palace, the masonry alone of the building costing him £80,000 sterling. The colonnade of the front elevation is of an architecture too fine, perhaps, for an individual and for a country house. The interior is full of rare marbles, and the walls of several rooms are covered with rare stucco work produced at great cost, and by workers brought from Italy.

Right up until the First World War, and in some cases beyond that period, servants were an integral part of big-house life in Ireland. They ensured a luxurious and leisured lifestyle for landlords by taking care of everything from caring for the richly furnished interiors of houses to cultivating extensive and elaborate gardens. The larger the house, the larger the number of servants required to cope with the number of tasks involved. In 1911, the Marquess of Conyhgham, for example, employed a private nurse, a governess, two lady's maids, a butler, cook, housekeeper, valet, two footmen, a hall boy, as well as scullery, kitchen, parlour, dairy and house maids at Slane. Recruitment of staff was usually through personal recommendations, particularly at the higher levels of house-keeper, governess and cook. Local Irish women found most opportunities for employment at the lower levels as maids in the house, kitchen, nursery or dairy. According to the 1871 census, domestic service accounted for almost 15 per cent of the female workforce. Certain families provided servants over several generations in the same house.

The English estate system had been introduced to Ulster during the Plantation and these estates were often on an enormous scale in order to establish effective local government as quickly as possible. This in turn ensured that almost all local government was placed in the hands of the landlord class, especially in Ulster where the estates were transformed into manors by the granting of royal patents. Tenants were granted security of tenure in the form of leases and compact enclosed farms became commonplace. The

First Marquis of Downshire, attributed to George Romney.

local landlord also had a major influence upon those who settled on his estates or established businesses in the nearest town. This can, of course, have a major impact on the variety and quality of records found in an estate collection. Arthur Brownlow, for example, allowed Presbyterians and Quakers to establish themselves in his town of Lurgan, County Armagh, at a time when both groups were regarded with suspicion by central government. As a result the records of both these groups for this area are of better quality and of great antiquity than is the case for much of Ulster. The Quaker records in particular date from the early seventeenth century.

Of course, many landlords are remembered with less affection. In south Armagh the local landowner Johnston of the Fews was determined to retain a firm grip on the local population. He established the village of Johnston Fews which he hoped would meet with the same success as many of the similar foundations of his neighbours. Four fairs were granted to the village. In 1740 it was described as a 'very small village in the middle of wild country called the Fews, notorious for robbers' and by the beginning of the nineteenth century it consisted of no more than six houses. The Johnston families' attempts to bring law and order to the district, which included the building of Fews Barracks, resulted in the famous couplet about them:

> Jesus of Nazareth, King of the Jews,
> Protect us from Johnston, the King of the Fews.

By the middle of the century more than three-quarters of the population lived in rural areas. Just over ½ million of these were tenants by the middle of the nineteenth century, and the vast majority of these held their land from year to year and had only a verbal agreement with their landlord. They could be evicted if they failed to pay their rents. Nevertheless, they were protected by customary rights built up over the years which gave them an interest in their property. Under tenant right, or Ulster Custom as it was known, the right of yearly tenants to undisturbed possession was accepted as long as they paid their rent. They could sell their interest in the property or pass it on to their heirs. Tenant right was accepted by landlords in Ulster and also in some other parts of the country.

For many tenants, particularly those with holdings of only a few acres, paying the rent depended upon access to income from other sources, such as peat-digging, domestic industry such as weaving or spinning, kelp collecting or seasonal work on the landlord estate. Most of them lived in a cottage supplied by their landlord and existed at a subsistence level because of high rentals and the competition for land and labour. The possibility of eviction remained an ever-present threat.

In the years before the Great Famine landlords used the threat of eviction to manage the tenants on their estates. When landlords intervened in family disputes, or in disputes between tenants, the notice to quit was their sanction – they could use it to threaten poachers, trespassers, drunkards, bad farmers, wife-beaters. Many used the process in moderation. Others abused the system: Lord Leitrim, for example, served all his tenants annually with notices to quit and kept them in a permanent state of insecurity.

A series of Land Acts followed culminating in the 1903 Act, popularly known as the Wyndam Act, which offered the landlords a 12 per cent bonus in addition to the agreed price if they agreed to sell out their entire estate. The Act also introduced the principle of sale of the whole estate, with tenants agreeing to common terms, rather than the piecemeal sale of holdings. Provision was also made for the purchase of estates by the Land Commission and the resale of untenanted lands to uneconomic holders or evicted tenants. The Act was popular with tenants because it guaranteed annual repayments lower than existing rents.

Therefore by the beginning of the twentieth century, government legislation had brought about in Ireland a complete revolution in land ownership. Within a generation the position of the landlords in Ireland had been altered as the land passed into the hands of the former tenants. 'The Act undid the confiscations of James I, Cromwell, and William III', as Nationalist MP Tim Healy, a supporter of the Wyndam Act, remarked. Between 1870 and 1933 tenants in what is now the Republic of Ireland bought out 450,000 holdings, a total of 15 million acres out of 17 million. The land question had, at last, been removed from Irish politics.

The administration of these estates produced a large quantity of records, including maps, rentals, account books, etc. Landed estate records, particularly the rent rolls that list the tenants on the estate, are a useful source of genealogical information. Although they do not often include details on the smallest tenants, due to the fact that most of these had no right of tenure, the records of the landed estates are of great importance as a result of the destruction of the nineteenth-century census returns.

Estate records can also include details of local towns that were often established as market centres by local landlords and who owned much of the property within the town boundary. Any researcher interested in family who migrated to Belfast during the early part of the nineteenth century, for example, should examine the papers of the Donegal estate. The same is true on a smaller scale for towns like Ballymena (the Adair estate), Hillsborough (Downshire), Downpatrick (Southwell), Cookstown (Stewart) and Strabane (Abercorn).

Most of the land held in Ulster during the three centuries that preceded the Land Purchase Acts was held by men who held patents from the Crown. These patents granted them rights and privileges over the lands they had been given and over their tenants. One of these privileges was the right to hold manorial courts: the court-baron, the court-leet, and the court of piepowder. The form of the court-baron that existed in Ulster until the mid-nineteenth century was the 'freeholders' court' which met every three weeks to try actions for debt, trepasses, etc. under 40s.

The court-leet was summoned twice a year by the steward or seneschal of the manor and everyone who owed suit to the lords' court was bound to attend. It dealt with a wide range of matters affecting the welfare of the manor boundaries, annoyances and nuisances, the condition of roads, streams and drains, false weights and measures, the regulation of the markets, the licensing of ale houses, the quality of bread and ale. The court-leet was able to levy fines and to commit a person to the pillory or the stocks, but it could not imprison anyone.

The court-leet book for the manor of Brownlow's Derry is a good example of the wide variety of genealogical information that this type of volume can contain. There are lists of jurors who met each May and November. One of their duties was to appoint individuals to various positions of responsibility and who were charged with enforcing the powers of the court-leet during the year. This included the 'Overseers for Regulating the size of Bread', the 'Regulaters of the Flesh Market, and such Wares and Commodities as are or may be exposed to Sale in the Town of Lurgan' and the appointment of 'Scavengers' and local

Antrim Castle, Illustrated Dublin Journal, *vol. 1, no. 14, 7 December 1861.*

constables. The following is an example from the court-leet book for the manor of Brownlow's Derry, dating from November 1776, of the jurors power to take action against local tenants who were proving a nuisance: 'We present the house in the Castle Lane lately occcupied by John Grimes to be a nuisance as dangerous to the lives of his Majesties Subjects, the front wall projecting out, and we direct the Seneschal will give directions to have the same pulled down unless the owner removes the danger in one month from this day.'(Brownlow Papers PRONI D/1928).

The name of the local landlord

If you do not know the name of the local landlord in a particular area you can normally find it by looking at the printed valuation books for 1860, which are available on the shelves of the Public Search Room and at most major libraries, where the landlord's name normally appears in the column headed 'lessor'.

Many of the great family estates were broken up in the latter years of the nineteenth century under the Land Acts, and by the Encumbered Estates Court. Before this happened a list of land owners was compiled, 1871–76, by government order and printed in the *Return of Owners of Land of One Acre and Upwards, in the Several Counties, Counties of Cities, and Counties of Towns in Ireland, to which is added A Summary For Each Province and for All of Ireland (Presented to both Houses of Parliament by Command of Her Majesty)*. The area measured covered more than 20 million acres and the number of owners of one or more acre was 32,614. An owner was defined as anyone who held title to the property outright or held a lease of more than 99 years, or a lease with the right of perpetual renewal. The names of owners are listed alphabetically by province and county and their addresses, the extent of their property and its valuation are also included.

The Ordnance Survey Memoirs, which were compiled in the 1830s, also provide useful information on the principal landowners across Northern Ireland before many estates changed hands in the mid-nineteenth century.

The records

The most important classes of records for family historians are:

Rentals

Rentals allow local historians to trace individual tenants and over a period of time show how one plot of land or property changed hands. Records were generally arranged by year (rents were usually paid half-yearly) or with several years covered by the same volume. The information provided will usually be limited to the name of the tenant, the extent and location of his holding and the rent payable by him.

Occasionally rentals are annotated with a change in occupancy, and the reason for it is sometimes given. Title deeds, although more cumbersome to use, include any documents that have been used to prove ownership to the property.

Leases

A landlord grants a lease to a tenant, who is given the right to occupy the property for a specific period of time. Two copies of the lease were usually prepared. The original lease was signed by the landlord and kept by the tenant. The counterpart was signed by the tenant and kept by the landlord. A lease was usually for a term of years, 1, 21, 50 or 99 years. The maximum term of a Roman Catholic lease was 31 years until the 1778 Act altered this.

In Ireland, as in the western half of England, leases were usually for three lives: the lease expired when all of the three persons named in the lease had died. The lease was stated to continue for 99 years or, if earlier, until the death of the last-named person. In a lease for lives the names of relatives are often included. The lease could be renewed at the fall of each life by inserting a new name on payment of a renewal fine. The three-life lease was therefore in reality in perpetuity as long as the tenant wished to renew it. Three-life leases are very useful for genealogists because a tenant frequently named members of his family (particularly sons and grandsons) as the lives. When new lives were inserted details of age and relationship were often included and it is possible to work out when the old life died.

Tenants often sublet the property, or part of it, to a third party; this was known as a sublease. The third party became an undertenant, paying rent to the tenant, who continued to pay rent to the landlord. A subtenant may not be picked up in the records of the estate, and this can be frustrating when you know that an ancestor leased land in a particular area. It is therefore worthwhile examining the correspondence between a landlord and his agent because this can be of immense genealogical value. Not only does it include details of the day-to-day running of the estate, but also mention is often made of those who worked on the estate.

Maps and plans

Maps and plans form an important element in most estate collections. These show the property of the landlord, who would have employed a surveyor to illustrate the extent of his land and the more important features on his estate. Maps come in all shapes and sizes and can be coloured or roughly sketched in black and white. Often there are blank spaces where the land does not belong to the surveyor's employer.

Surveys may include the names of tenants and the extent of their holdings. They give many place names that have long disappeared and show the location of vanished mills, woodland, paths and houses. They illustrate the method of agriculture employed in a particular area and the size of fields and holdings.

Evictions

Evictions and debt collections were very public affairs and often made the local press. Ejectment books contain a wealth of genealogical information: the names of hundreds of tenants, the location of the farms and sometimes details of the lease. Ejectment books can be found in estate collections held by the National Library and National Archives, Dublin, and the Public Record Office of Northern Ireland.

Other classes of records

Landlords or estate agents often kept tithe lists, voters' lists, seventeenth-century muster rolls, and notes concerning family alliances and the character of various tenants.

Stock returns, 1803

One of the most interesting set of records held within an estate collection at PRONI are the stock returns of 1803. With rumours of an anticipated French invasion of Ireland, a remarkable series of returns of live and dead stock were made for more than forty maritime parishes in County Down. Each parish return is arranged by townland and the details for each include the names of individuals with locations, the number of farm animals they had, the extent of their crops and details of carriages they owned. For some parishes there is also an additional column noting the 'names of men willing and able to serve', particularly blacksmiths and skilled craftsmen. These returns are in the Londonderry Estate papers PRONI reference, D/654/A2.

Parish of Newry

Desart Townland:	Isaac Glenny	1 cow, 2 young cattle
Crowreagh Townland:	John Glenny	2 cows, 1 young cattle
Loughorne Townland:	Messrs. Glenny	No livestock
Savilmore Townland:	Isaac Glenny Esq.	3 cows, 9 young cattle, 9 sheep/goats, 6 pigs
Boat Street, Newry:	Isaac Wm.Glenny	3 cows

Agricultural Census, 1803, PRONI ref: D/654/A2/29.

Irish Land Commission

The Land Commission was set up in 1881 under the Land Act of that year. Its main function became the advancement of money to tenants to enable them to purchase their holdings and the fixing of fair rents under the various Land Acts from 1881 onwards. Because the Commission had to be satisfied that potential purchasers would be able to repay their annuities it employed inspectors to assess the capacity of tenants to make their repayments. Therefore, the Land Commission records are one of the few sources that reveal as much about the tenants as about landlords.

The records of the Irish Land Commission concerning sales of estates in Northern Ireland to tenants were transferred from Dublin to Belfast in 1922 and were subsequently deposited in the Land Registry archive (ref LR/1) at Public Record Office of Northern Ireland. The Land Registry archive, which contains an estimated 50,000 items, is one of the largest held in PRONI and contains numerous classes of records that will be of interest to genealogists. Title deeds, for example, relate to the tenure of property, including its origin, length of lease and other conditions under which the lease was held. These often include papers from the eighteenth and early nineteenth centuries which recite names of people formerly associated with the property. Testamentary papers include wills and other testamentary material which should prove to be useful to research of a genealogical nature.

There are three indexes that can be used to identify documents likely to be of interest to researchers:

Mount Hall, Narrow Water, Warrenpoint, Ulster Folk and Transport Museum, WAG/3451.

- Alphabetical index, by name of estate;
- Numerical index by record number;
- Numerical index by box number.

Another way for the family historian to access the records of the Irish Land Commission is through the pages of the local newspapers. The sittings of the Land Courts were reported in considerable detail. These include the cases of individual tenants who placed their cases before the Commissioners. The Commissioners' decisions are often followed by a list of tenants with the old rent and the new judicial rent given. Lists such as these can provide evidence that an ancestor lived on a particular estate towards the end of the nineteenth century.

The Commissioners' decisions are often followed by a list of tenants with the old rent and the new judicial rent given. Lists such as these can provide evidence that an ancestor lived on a particular estate towards the end of the nineteenth century.

ENNISKILLEN SUB-COMMISSION
At Enniskillen Courthouse, on Tuesday, Ulick Bourke, Esq.,
Legal Commissioner, and Mr Wm Davidson, sat and delivered judgement
in several cases.
The following professional gentlemen attended – Messers Joseph Alexander,
John Graham, J W Dane, George Knight, CERA Irvine, and J C Macniffe.
The following were the awards ——
Colonel J J Irvine, landlord

Tenant	Area	Old Rent	Valn	Jud. Rent
	a r p	£ s d	£ s d	£ s d
Rose Monaghan	15 1 20	9 16 0	8 5 0	—
Thomas M'Caffrey	20 3 0	12 10 0	11 0 0	—
Catherine Maguire	47 1 20	16 8 0	14 15 0	12 10 0
Mick Muldoon	16 0 14	12 0 0	8 10 0	7 10 0
Edward Henigan	20 0 0	12 0 0	19 5 0	7 10 0
Patrick Muldoon	24 3 8	11 10 0	9 10 0	8 0 0
Owen McQuade	18 0 0	7 0 0	6 5 0	5 12 0
Edward McHugh	20 2 12	5 12 0	5 5.0	4 0 0
W H Archdale, landlord				
Isabella Muldoon	9 3 32	13 15 0	—	9 0 0

Extract from the *Fermanagh Times*, 7 December 1882.

The *Guide to Landed Estate Records* in PRONI contains an index to the Land Registry papers.

Church Temporalities

The Land Purchase Commission archive includes Church Temporalities files and deeds. The Irish Church Act 1869, which disestablished the Church of Ireland, also vested its property in a body of Commissioners, known as the Commissioners of Church Temporalities in Ireland. This body was empowered to lend money to the tenants to enable them to purchase their land. Subsequently, the interests and powers of the Commissioners in respect of property in Northern Ireland were transferred to the Ministry of Finance.

On the winding up of the Commission various records were deposited at PRONI. These included the records of the Commissioners of Crown Lands, for whom the Land Purchase Commission acted under an interdepartmental arrangement. The Crown Estate Commissioners archive (PRONI ref CL) includes title deeds that frequently include the names of the original tenant copied from the ancient Crown Rent Rolls; the Arrears Files include extracts from the Down Survey and Distribution Books or Rent Rolls which include the names of the original owner and details of earlier payments of the Quit Rents. The files of the Land Judges Court usually include the names of the immediate lessors and occupiers and, on occasion, a list of tenants on the estate and corresponding maps may be found.

Registry of Deeds

The Registry of Deeds was established by an Act of Parliament in 1708. The aim of the Act was to provide one central office in Dublin 'for the public registering of all deeds, conveyances and wills, that shall be made of any honours, manors, lands, tenements or hereditaments'. Researchers must remember that the Act establishing the Registry of Deeds had its origin in the penal laws. From 1704 to 1780 no Catholic could purchase a lease for more than thirty-one years nor could a Catholic invest in mortgages. Also landowners were often apathetic about officially registering leases with their tenants, particularly those on smallholdings.

There are over 4 million memorials stored in the Registry of Deeds archive dealing with property in Ireland from its establishment. A memorial is a summary of a deed, and a description of the property and its location. Memorials are more often than not sufficiently detailed to substitute for the original documents that may no longer be in existence.

Registration was not compulsory, and the number of deeds recorded varied from place to place. The deeds registered include leases, mortgages, marriage settlements and wills. This can provide the researcher with names, addresses and occupations of the parties involved as well as the names of those who acted as witness. During registration, which often took place years after the original transaction, a copy of the deed called a memorial was made. The details of the memorial were then copied into a large bound volume. It is these transcript volumes that are available for public inspection.

The types of deeds most commonly met with are leases, mortgages, marriage settlements and rent charges. The value of leases to the genealogist is explained below, in the section on landed estates. Only leases for longer than three years could be registered at the Registry of Deeds.

A marriage settlement was the agreement made between the families of the prospective bride and groom prior to their wedding. The main aim was to provide financial security to the woman should she outlive her husband. The information in this type of deed varies, but can include the names and addresses of a large number of people from the two families involved. Occasionally the more detailed settlements include lists of names of tenants living on the lands of the groom's family.

In the era before banks were widespread, mortgages were commonly used as a ready means of raising capital, particularly by merchants and those seeking to buy land. They are not always easy to identify and their genealogical value can be fairly limited. Rent charges were annual payments issuing from nominated lands and were used to pay off debts or provide for those family members without an adequate income.

A large number of wills were registered. A will was usually registered if there were concerns that it was going to be contested. Abstracts of over 2,000 wills registered between 1708 and 1832 were published in 3 volumes by the Irish Manuscripts Commission (P B Phair and E Ellis (eds), *Abstracts of Wills at the Registry of Deeds (1954–88)*).

Each registered deed was given its own individual reference number. In the indexes to the deeds the volume and the page are also given. For example, the reference 18.236.8764 means that this particular deed is on page 236 of volume 18 and is deed number 8764. This referencing system was used until 1832. After that the reference number includes the year in which the deed was registered.

Two indexes are available to the researcher: the Index of Grantors and a Lands Index. The format of the Index of Grantors has changed over the years. Before 1832 the Index gives the surname and the Christian name of the grantor, the surname of the grantee and the reference number. There is no indication of the location of the property concerned. After 1832 the Index is more detailed and includes the county in which the property is located.

The Lands Index is arranged by county, with one or more counties per volume: the entries are arranged alphabetically, but only with regard to initial letter. Each entry gives the surnames of the parties, the name of the denomination of land and the reference number. After 1828 the Lands Index is subdivided by barony. Additional references were often put at the end of books.

The Registry of Deeds is located in a large Georgian building in Henrietta Street, Dublin. PRONI has microfilms of both the indexes and the deeds (MIC/7 and MIC/311). A good guide to the Registry of Deeds is Jean Agnew, 'How to use the Registry of Deeds' in *Familia*, vol. 2, no. 6 (1990).

Encumbered estates

The Great Famine had a massive impact on the management and economic viability of landed estates. Many estates were mortgaged and landowners unable to collect rents were forced to sell their estates. Some landlords had to sell parts of their estates to remain solvent. By an Act of Parliament in 1849 an Encumbered Estates Court was established with authority to sell estates on the application of the owner or encumbrancer (one who had a claim on the estate). After the sale the court distributed the money among the creditors and granted clear title to the new owners. The Landed Estates Court assumed the functions of the court in 1853.

Edenderry market house and main street, 1858, PRONI D/671.

Between 1849 and 1857 over 3,000 Irish estates were sold to approximately 3,200 purchasers.

Printed rentals or particulars of sale were issued before the sale of a property and therefore contain very detailed information on tenants and holdings on each estate in order to attract potential buyers. They are divided into counties, townlands and tenements and feature the names of the parties involved and the date. Included are rentals, maps of the estate giving tenants' names and, on occasion, surveys of the estate. Many landlords owned properties in local towns and villages, and these too can be found in the Encumbered Estates Rentals. Before 1862, the maps were usually the work of valuators, but after that date they were official Ordnance Survey maps.

The Irish Encumbered Estates Rentals are in bound volumes and are available for the whole of Ireland. They are divided into counties, townlands or house and tenements, the names of the parties involved and the date. Included are rentals, maps of the estate giving tenants names and, on occasion, surveys of the estate. They are an under-used source for genealogists interested in the names of tenants of various estates throughout Ireland in the mid-nineteenth century, PRONI D/1201.

A basic index to Encumbered Estates Court is available on the PRONI Search Room shelves.

Chapter 11

WILLS AND TESTAMENTARY RECORDS

Once the date of death of an ancestor has been discovered, it is worth finding out whether they left a will. Wills contain not only the name, address and occupation of the testator, but also details of the larger family network, such as cousins and nephews. Many wills also include the addresses and occupations of the beneficiaries, witnesses and executors. Before the 1882 Married Women's Property Act married women rarely made wills as all their possessions, even their clothes, in law belonged to their husbands. Therefore, wills before 1883 were mostly made by widows and spinsters and even after this date they are not very numerous until the 1940s and 1950s.

One should not assume that because the family was too poor they would not have made a will. Sometimes those who made the will were determined that it went to the right person when they died. Strangely it doesn't always follow that people who were in comfortable positions left wills. People from well-to-do families sometimes disposed of their wealth before they died in order to avoid death duties. If a person dies without making a will, he/she is described as intestate. In this case, the Court of Probate will usually appoint administrators and can grant letters of administration to the next of kin or to the principal creditor to administer the estate of the intestate.

Between 1536 and 1858, the Church of Ireland was responsible for all wills and administrations in Ireland. The Probate Act of 1857 transferred probate authority from the Church of Ireland to the newly founded government probate districts. The Church of Ireland subsequently transferred their wills and administrations to the Public Record Office in Dublin. Most wills from before 1900 – some dating from the early sixteenth century – were destroyed when, in 1922, the Public Record Office was bombed during the Irish Civil War. Luckily, will indexes and administration indexes survived and copies of most wills after 1858 were preserved.

In addition, Sir William Betham, as Ulster King of Arms, 1820–53, superintended the construction of alphabetical indexes and also drew up brief genealogical abstracts of almost all those wills that pre-dated 1800. He later constructed sketch pedigrees from his notes. The original note-books in which he recorded the information are now in the NAI, and The Genealogical Office, Dublin, has his sketch pedigrees based on these abstracts and including later additions and amendments. The Genealogical Office transcript copy (GO 257–260) is fully alphabetical, unlike the notebooks. PRONI has in its custody a later copy of Burke's volumes of pedigrees and small 'family trees' compiled from almost all pre-1858 prerogative wills, to which there is a typescript catalogue Index T/559.

Wills before 1858

Prior to 1858 the Church of Ireland was responsible for administering all testamentary affairs. Ecclesiastical or Consistorial Courts in each diocese were responsible for granting probate and conferring on the executors the power to administer the estate. Each court was responsible for wills and administrations in its own diocese. You can use Brian Mitchell's *A New Genealogical Atlas of Ireland*, which has county maps that associate civil parishes with Church of Ireland dioceses, to identify the diocese in which your ancestor lived. Researchers should also bear it mind that when the estate included property worth more than £5 in another diocese, responsibility for the will or administration passed to the Prerogative Court under the authority of the Archbishop of Armagh.

Indexes to those wills destroyed in 1922 are available on the shelves of the Search Rooms at PRONI. In addition, many thousands of copies of wills probated before 1858 have been collected over the years by PRONI. A card index for pre-1858 surviving wills and will abstracts is also available in the Public Search Room at PRONI. This is arranged alphabetically by the name of the testator and provides the references to wills or extracts from wills that are scattered throughout PRONI collections. Altogether PRONI has over 13,000 copies and abstracts of pre-1858 wills.

Some indexes have been published. The most important is the *Index to Prerogative Wills, 1536–1810*, edited by Sir Arthur Vicars and published in 1897. This very important reference work for genealogists lists the full name, residence, title or occupation and date of probate for almost 40,000 names. It is a particularly important index for the Irish researcher because it serves as a guide to the names that can be found in *Betham's Abstracts*. You can also consult the Eneclann CD-ROM, *Indexes to Irish Wills, 1484–1858*, which can be purchased online at Ancestry.com or at: www.eneclann.ie. This CD-ROM contains over 70,000 entries from surviving wills, administrations, transcriptions and abstracts.

Wills, 1858–1900

From 1858 district probate courts took over responsibility for wills and administrations from the Church of Ireland. The twelve probate registries created at the time were: the Principal Registry in Dublin and eleven district registries in Armagh, Ballina, Belfast, Cavan, Cork, Kilkenny, Limerick, Londonderry, Mullingar, Tuam and Waterford. The wills of wealthier members of society tended to be probated at the Principal Registry.

The district registries retained transcripts of the wills that they proved and of the administrations intestate that they granted before the annual transfer of the original records (20 or more years old) to the Public Record office of Ireland in Dublin. The original wills were destroyed in Dublin in 1922 but the transcripts copies in will books survived. Those for Northern Ireland are now on deposit in PRONI where they are available on micro-film for the period 1858–1900 (MIC/15C). Each volume contains an alphabetical index.

Belfast and Northern Counties Railway terminus, York Road, Belfast, Lawrence Collection.

There is not a comprehensive index to these post-1858 wills and grants. However, there are bound annual indexes called 'calendars' at PRONI. These calendars are of value to genealogists since they provide the name, address, occupation and date of death of the testator as well as the names, addresses and occupations of executors, the value of estate and the place and date of probate. Even if you have only an approximate date for the death of an ancestor it is worth looking through a number of volumes in the hope of spotting an entry giving details of their will.

When using these calendars to gain access to a will or transcript, the vital date to note is not the date when the will was signed or the date of death. It is the date of probate, i.e., the date when it was officially proved in a probate registry. This date of probate is normally a few months after a person died. However, it is well to bear in mind that a significant number of wills were probated ten or more years after death. Such delays may have been more common where probate was in the Principal Registry in Dublin.

An index to the will calendar entries (grants of probate and letters of administration) is now available on the PRONI website at: www.proni.gov.uk. This website is the first phase of a project to index and digitise all the early wills that were proved in the District Probate Registries of Armagh, Belfast and Londonderry from 1858 to c. 1900. It provides a fully searchable index to the will calendar entries for these three District Probate Registries with the facility to view the entire will calendar entry for each successful search.

PRONI also has a card index to post-1858 surviving wills and will abstracts. This index is most useful when looking for a copy or abstract of a will probate at the Principal Registry in Dublin, which would have been destroyed in 1922 without a transcript being made.

Wills from 1900

PRONI has in its custody all wills for the districts of Belfast and Londonderry from 1900 to, at present, the mid-1990s, and Armagh from 1900 until it closed in 1921. After 1900 the original wills and their associated papers are available filed in a separate envelope for each testator. If the person did not make a will there may be letters of administration that give the name, residence and occupation of the deceased as well as the name and address of the person or persons appointed to administer the estate. Post-1900 wills are found by using the annual will calendars located in the reception area at PRONI.

An index to printed Irish will calendars 1878–1900, which includes surname and first name of testator, county or overseas country of residence and death, date of death and year of probate on around 151,000 individuals for all of Ireland, is available to members of the Ulster Genealogical and Historical Guild at: www.ancestryireland.com/database.php?filename=db_wills.

Chapter 12

PRINTED SOURCES

Ordnance Survey Memoirs

In 1824 a House of Commons committee recommended a townland survey of Ireland with maps at the scale of 6in to 1 statute mile to facilitate a uniform valuation for local taxation. The survey was directed by Colonel Thomas Colby, who had available to him officers of the Royal Engineers and three companies of sappers and miners. In addition, civil servants were recruited to help with sketching, drawing and engraving maps and eventually, in the 1830s, with the writing of the memoirs.

Ordnance Survey Memoirs provide a great deal of background information on the character and habits of the people who lived in Ireland during the early part of the nineteenth century.

The memoirs were written descriptions intended to accompany the maps, containing information that could not be fitted on to them. They are a unique source for the history of the northern half of Ireland before the Great Famine, as they document the landscape and situation, buildings and antiquities, land-holdings and population, employment and livelihoods of the parishes. The surveyors recorded the habits of the people, their food, drink, dress and customs. Details of ruined churches, prehistoric monuments and standing stones were also included.

The Ordnance Survey Memoirs contain much valuable information on ancient forts, settlements and graveyards. Of particular interest to the local historian is the information on local schools, churches and landed estates as well as descriptions of the towns and villages. Useful genealogical information can also be found. The memoirs for the parish Hillsborough, County Down, for example, contain an extensive list of subscribers to the Hillsborough Charitable Society, which sought to provide food, clothing and shelter for the destitute poor.

Fascinating insights into the everyday life of our ancestors are provided with descriptions of local dress or customs. Some information on local names can occasionally be found.

Only the northern part of Ireland was covered before the scheme was dropped. In recent years the Institute of Irish Studies at The Queen's University of Belfast has published the Ordnance Survey Memoirs in forty volumes as follows:

- County Antrim: vols 2, 8, 10, 13, 16, 19, 21, 23, 24, 26, 29, 32, 35 and 37;

- County Armagh: vol. 1;

- County Donegal: vols 38 and 39;

- County Down: vols 3, 7, 12 and 17;

- County Fermanagh: vols 4 and 14;

- County Londonderry: vols 6, 9, 11, 15, 18, 22, 25, 27, 28, 30, 31, 33, 34 and 36;

- County Tyrone: vols 5 and 20.

Street directories and almanacs

Street directories contain a great deal of information on the gentry, the professional classes, merchants, etc. They include information on even the smallest of market towns and ports in Ireland. Beginning with a description of the town and surrounding countryside, the names and addresses of the local butchers, pawnbrokers, blacksmiths and coach-builders are given, as well as the various places of worship, with the names of the local ministers, etc. and the location of local schools. Street directories can therefore be useful if you wish to find out which church or school your ancestor attended. The names and addresses of the local Members of Parliament, magistrates, Poor Law Guardians and town commissioners are also included in many street directories. In fact, the only classes that are excluded from directories are the small tenant farmers, landless labourers and servants.

PRONI has recently made its pre-1901 street directories accessible and fully searchable online at: http://streetdirectories.proni.gov.uk. This is a very welcome initiative allowing family historians to search thirty directories under a particular name or location. It also has microfilmed copies of the rare works. PRONI has a large collection of directories available in its Public Search Room.

Benburb Castle, Tyrone, Atlas and Cyclopedia of Ireland, 1900.

Countrywide directories

Ambrose Leet's *A Director to the Market Towns, Villages, Gentlemen's Seats, and other Noted Places in Ireland*, 1814, was one of the first general directories for all of Ireland. The principal countrywide directories that are invaluable to family historians are those published by James Pigot, Alexander Thom and J Slater. Pigot's *Commercial Directory of Ireland, Scotland etc* was published in 1820; a subsequent edition was produced in 1824.

Thom's Irish Almanac and Official Directory, published from 1844, annually until 1915, lists all Members of Parliament, the Irish peerage, baronets and officers of the Army, Navy and Militia, as well as members of government departments, all county officers, members of professional organisations and the professions of law, medicine, surgery, bankers, etc. The clergy of all denominations are listed under the churches, and the dioceses, towns, and districts, according to the Church ecclesiastical organisation. Officers of universities, colleges, schools, etc. are also named. In fact, the lists cover all but the gentry, who filled no public or professional place, the tradesmen, small farmers and the lower classes.

Slater's *National Commercial Directory of Ireland*, 1846, 1856, 1870, 1881 and 1894, contains an Index to the Provinces, Counties, and the Cities, Post and Market Towns of Ireland. The directory is arranged under the four provinces. Each city, post and market town is represented with a list of its nobility, gentry and clergy. Members of all professions and trades are listed separately except under the smallest towns, for which they are grouped alphabetically with their occupations designated. In addition, for Dublin, Belfast and Limerick, there is an 'alphabetical directory' of the city and its suburbs, containing the names, occupation and address of every man listed in the classified section. Also included at the back of the volume are classified directories of the principal merchants, manufacturers and traders of seven English cities and of Glasgow and Paisley, Scotland.

Provincial directories

During the nineteenth century, a great many local directories were produced particularly for important commercial centres such as Belfast, Londonderry and Newry, although the quality of these vary considerably from locality to locality. Those of particular interest to anyone planning on tracing his or her family tree will now be considered.

A wide range of directories are available for Belfast. These include *Martin's Belfast Directory*, 1839 and 1841–42, which features an alphabetical list of gentry, merchants and traders living in Belfast and also a street-by-street listing of the principal streets. Matier's *Belfast Directory*, 1835–36 and *c.* 1860, includes an alphabetical list of gentry, merchants and traders residing in Belfast and its neighbourhood. The *Belfast and Province of Ulster Directory*, published various years from 1854 to 1947, has a street-by-street listing for Belfast. The principal towns are represented with alphabetical lists of gentry, merchants and traders, and the principal villages of Ulster consist of alphabetical lists of 'residents in vicinity'. Henderson's *Belfast and Province of Ulster Directory*, 1843–44, 1846–47, 1849 and 1852 includes a street-by-street listing and an alphabetical list of the 'principal inhabitants'.

Some of the more valuable directories are listed below.

Belfast

1805: *Holden's Annual London and Country Directory of the United Kingdom & Wales*
1807–1808: *Smyth & Lyons Belfast Directories*
1811: *Holden's Annual London and Country Directory of the United Kingdom & and Wales*
1813: *Belfast Street Directory*
1816: *Holden's Annual Directory Class Second*
1819: *Belfast General and Commercial Directory* by Thomas Bradshaw
1820: *Smyth's Directory to Belfast and Vicinity*
1831–32: *Donaldson's Belfast Directory*
1835–36: *Matier's Belfast Directory*
1839, 1840, 1841, 1842: *Martin's Belfast Directories*
1843–44: *Henderson's New Belfast Directory*
1843–44: *Post-Office Belfast Annual Directory*
1846, 1850, 1852: *Henderson's Belfast Directories*
1846, 1856, 1870: *Slater's National Commercial Directories of Ireland*
1852: *Belfast and Province of Ulster Directory* – by volume to 1894 then annually

1860–61: *Adair's Belfast Directory*
1870: *Belfast and Province of Ulster Post-Office Directory*
1881, 1894: *Slater's Royal National Commercial Directories of Ireland*
1887: *Belfast Directory* (vol. XII in BPUD series)
1894: *Slater's Royal National Commercial Directory of Belfast and its Suburbs*
1902, 1905, 1909, 1913: *Macdonald's Irish Directory and Gazetteer*

A comprehensive set of Belfast directories (many including details of provincial towns) is available online at the Lennon Wylie website at: ww.lennonwylie.co.uk/.

Country Antrim

1816: *Holden's Annual Directory Class Second*
1819: *Belfast General and Commercial Directory* by Thomas Bradshaw, Belfast
1824: *Pigot & Co's City of Dublin & Hibernian Provincial Directory*
1846, 1856, 1870: *Slater's National Commercial Directories of Ireland*
1852: *Belfast and Province of Ulster Directory* – by volume to 1894 then annual
1861: *Coleraine Almanac and Directory*
1881, 1894: *Slater's Royal National Commercial Directories of Ireland*
1884: *Coleraine Almanack*
1886: *Wood's Coleraine & Portrush Directory*
1888: *Bassett's Book of Antrim*
1889: *Ballymena and mid-Antrim Directory*
1892: *Boyd's Larne Almanac*
1893: *MacNeill's Lisburn Directory*
1894: *Business . . . Directory for Lisburn*
1901: *Derry and Antrim Year Book*
1902, 1905, 1909, 1913: *Macdonald's Irish Directory and Gazetteer*

Country Armagh

1816: *Holden's Annual Directory Class Second*
1819: *The General Directory of Newry, Armagh . . .* by Thomas Bradshaw
1824: *Pigot & Co's City of Dublin & Hibernian Provincial Directory*
1840: *The New Commercial Directory of Armagh, Newry, Londonderry . . .*
1846, 1856, 1870: *Slater's National Commercial Directories of Ireland*
1852: *Belfast and Province of Ulster Directory* – by volume to 1894 then annually
1873: *City of Armagh Directory*
1876: *County Armagh Almanack and Directory*

1881, 1894: *Slater's Royal National Commercial Directories of Ireland*
1883: *County Armagh Directory and Almanac* by S Farrell
1888: *Bassett's Book of County Armagh*
1888: *White's Lurgan Directory*
1902, 1905, 1909, 1913: *Macdonald's Irish Directory and Gazetteer*

County Down

1811: *Holden's Annual London and Country Directory, of the United Kingdom &
Wales*
1816: *Holden's Annual Directory Class Second*
1819: *The General Directory of Newry, Armagh . . .* by Thomas Bradshaw
1824: *Pigot & Co's City of Dublin & Hibernian Provincial Directory*
1839: *MacCabe's Directory of Newry*
1840: *The New Commercial Directory of Armagh, Newry, Londonderry . . .*
1846, 1856, 1870: *Slater's National Commercial Directories of Ireland*
1852: *Belfast and Province of Ulster Directory* – by volume to 1894 then
annually
1862: *Directory of Newcastle, Newry, Newtownards*
1868: *Wylys Directory Newry and Warrenpoint*
1874: *Banbridge Household Almanack*
1875: *Newtownards and County Down Illustrated Almanac and Directory*
1876: *Directory and Guidebook for Newry, Bessbrook, Warrenpoint . . .*
1878: *Down Recorder Household Almanac and Local and County Directory*
1881: *Lyttle's North Down Almanac and Directory*
1881, 1894: *Slater's Royal National Commercial Directories of Ireland*
1886: *Bassett's County Down (One Hundred Years Ago)*
1902, 1905, 1909, 1913: *Macdonald's Irish Directory and Gazetteer*

County Fermanagh

1824: *Pigot & Co's City of Dublin & Hibernian Provincial Directory*
1848: *The Handbook or Directory, for the County of Fermanagh* by C Macloskie
1846, 1856, 1870: *Slater's National Commercial Directories of Ireland*
1852: *Belfast and Province of Ulster Directory* – by volume to 1894 then
annually
1880: *Lowe's Fermanagh Directory & Household Almanac*
1881, 1894: *Slater's Royal National Commercial Directories of Ireland*
1896: *Omagh Almanac, Tyrone, Fermanagh and Donegal Directory*
1902, 1905, 1909, 1913: *Macdonald's Irish Directory and Gazetteer*

County Londonderry

1816: *Holden's Annual Directory Class Second*
1824: *Pigot & Co's City of Dublin & Hibernian Provincial Directory*
1839: *A New Directory of the City of Londonderry . . .*
1840: *The New Commercial Directory of Armagh, Newry, Londonderry . . .*
1846, 1856, 1870: *Slater's National Commercial Directories of Ireland*
1852: *Belfast and Province of Ulster Directory 1852* – by vol. to 1894 then annually
1881, 1894: *Slater's Royal National Commercial Directories of Ireland*
1884: *Coleraine Almanack*
1884: *Derry Almanac*
1890: *Derry Almanac and North-West Directory*
1901: *Derry and Antrim Year Book*
1902, 1905, 1909, 1913: *Macdonald's Irish Directory and Gazetteer*

County Tyrone

1816: *Holden's Annual Directory Class Second*
1824: *Pigot & Co's City of Dublin & Hibernian Provincial Directory*
1846, 1856, 1870: *Slater's National Commercial Directories of Ireland*
1852: *Belfast and Province of Ulster Directory* – by volume to 1894 then annually

General/Ulster

1805: *Holden's Annual London and Country Directory of the United Kingdom & Wales*
1811: *Holden's Annual London and Country Directory, of the United Kingdom & Wales*
1816: *Holden's Annual Directory Class Second*
1820–21: *(Pigot's) The Commercial Directory of Ireland*
1824: *Pigot & Co's City of Dublin & Hibernian Provincial Directory*
1843–44: *Henderson's New Belfast Directory*
1843–44: *Post Office Belfast Annual Directory*
1846, 1856, 1870: *Slater's National Commercial Directories of Ireland*
1852: *Belfast and Province of Ulster Directory* – by volume to 1894 then annually
1852: *Slater's Trades Directory*
1865: *(Wynne's) Business Directory of Belfast and Principal Towns in the Province of Ulster*
1870: *Belfast & Province of Ulster Post-Office Directory*

1878: *Belfast and District Directory, and Ulster Guide*
1881, 1894: *Slater's Royal National Commercial Directories of Ireland*
1893: *Belfast and Northern Counties Directory*
1902, 1905, 1909, 1913: *Macdonald's Irish Directory and Gazetteer*
1908: *Belfast and Ulster Towns' Directory*

For more information on the large number of directories available see James Carty's *National Library of Ireland Bibliography of Irish History, 1870–1911* (Dublin, 1940) and Edward Evans' *Historical and Bibliographical Account of Almanacks, Directories etc. in Ireland from the Sixteenth Century* (Dublin, 1897), which include details of provincial directories.

Newspapers

Newspapers have been published in Ireland since the mid-seventeenth century. The oldest newspaper in the National Library's collection is *An Account of Chief Occurrences in Ireland*, published in February 1660 by Sir Charles Coote. It only ran for a few issues. The *Newsletter*, which was published in Dublin in 1685 and appeared twice a week for seven months, is closer to the modern concept of newspaper publication.

The first newspapers were published in the seventeenth century, but it was not until the eighteenth century that the larger towns began to publish their own newspapers. These early newspapers can prove disappointing for local historians because they concentrated mainly on national and international news. Local news only began to feature later in the eighteenth century. They are useful, nevertheless, because they feature advertisements, obituaries, market prices and properties to let. By the early nineteenth century newspapers had become the most important medium of public opinion and information. At the same time, local newspapers increasingly covered local issues. Births, deaths and marriages were covered more frequently and, like obituaries, these usually related to the higher echelons of society.

Newspapers can on occasion provide descriptions of people that would not be found in more official records, as the following extract from the *Belfast News-Letter*, 7 February 1800, shows:

DESCRIPTION OF ARCHER

THOMAS ARCHER, for whose Apprehension a — Reward of ONE HUNDRED POUNDS is offered is a Deserter from the Antrim Militia — about 5 Feet 6 Inches high — Dark Complexion — Black Hair — Gray Eyes — Smooth-faced — rather Slender — by Trade a Shoemaker — has a long Chin — marked with Small Pox a little, and not very deeply.

The stocks,
Dromore, c. 1915,
Ulster Folk and
Transport
Museum, WAG/
1193.

Newspapers can also provide interesting gossip about the transgressions or troubles of an ancestor, as shown in this example from the *Fermanagh News*, 5 May 1904:

> The action was brought by Miss Ellen Price, aged 22 years, who resides in County Fermanagh, to recover damages for alleged breach of promise of marriage from Thomas Robert Thompson, a small farmer resident in the same county. Counsel referred to an affidavit of the plantiff, who stated that from the month of November, 1902, until recently defendant had been paying her attention, and had called at the house of her uncle, where she was living, and taken her out to walk and to church. The affidavit further stated that seduction took place under promise of marriage, and in March last a child was born.

The defendant denied all charges, both parties being described by counsel as being 'in humble circumstances'. The case was adjourned.

Identifying newspapers

The drawback in using newspapers for genealogy is that you generally need to have a fairly precise date for an event before you start hunting for coverage, since indexes are limited. If you have the date of a marriage or a trail or a fatal accident you first need to find what newspapers were being published at the time in the relevant area. For this the essential source is

Newsplan Project in Ireland (London and Dublin, 1992), compiled by James O'Toole. This lists all newspapers published in Ireland with their dates of operation. It also has chronological lists of newspapers arranged by town of publication and by county, so it is easy to identify which papers were in existence in an area at a given time. Remember, however, to check under the names of adjoining counties, as local newspapers never respected invisible county boundaries. The Newsplan database is available online at: www.nli.ie/newsplan/default.htm.

Local newspapers can be consulted in public libraries. They are often available only on microfilm and if you are lucky may have been indexed locally. The Linen Hall Library, Belfast, has an index to births, marriages and deaths in the *Belfast News-Letter*, covering the years 1738–1864. Belfast Central Library holds a series of fully indexed cuttings books of articles derived from major local newspapers since 1898. The microfilm of this series spans the years 1898–1976. From 1976 the newspaper cutting books are held in hard copy in the Irish and Local Studies Department.

Chapter 13

POOR LAW RECORDS

During the nineteenth century the Irish Poor Law was the British government's main instrument of social policy for dealing with Ireland's many social problems. The chief aim of this policy was to establish a system of indoor relief through a series of workhouses into which the destitute could be interned out of sight behind the workhouse walls. However, the Great Famine radically altered the system as laid down in 1838, establishing as it did the principle of outdoor relief, which ensured that the Poor Law would become the foundation of both Northern and Southern Ireland's social services.

Ireland was divided into 137 Poor Law Unions. These ignored traditional divisions, such as the county, barony and parish, and were centred on a market town where a workhouse was built. The Boards of Guardians were instructed to discourage all but the most needy paupers from applying to the workhouse for assistance. The workhouse was administered on behalf of local rate payers by the local Boards of Guardians. In their *Sixth Annual Report*, the Poor Law Commissioners admitted that it was no easy task to make conditions in the workhouse sufficiently bleak that it would deter only the most destitute:

> It must be obvious to anyone conversant with the habits and mode of living of the Irish people that to establish a dietary in the workhouse inferior to the ordinary diet of the poor classes would be difficult, if not, in many cases, impossible; and hence it has been contended that the workhouse system of relief is inapplicable to Ireland.

The harshness of the conditions within the workhouse can also be seen in the records. It was a fundamental rule of the workhouse system that 'no individual capable of exertion must ever be permitted to be idle in a workhouse and to allow none who are capable of employment to be idle at any time'. The men were employed breaking stones, grinding corn, working on the land attached to the workhouse or at other manual work about the house; the women at house duties, mending clothes, washing, attending the children and the sick, as well as manual work including breaking stones. The Master of the workhouse was empowered to punish any pauper for a whole range of misdemeanours, which included 'Making any noise when silence is ordered', 'Not duly cleansing his person' and 'Playing at cards or any game of chance'. Punishments included breaking stones for a week, going without shoes for a week and being flogged. More serious offences were dealt with by the civil authorities. According to the regulations workhouse food 'must on no account be superior or even equal to the ordinary mode of subsistence of the labouring classes of the neighbourhood'.

They were forced to rely on the 'regularity, order, strict enforcement of cleanliness, constant occupation, the preservation of decency and decorum, and exclusion of any of the irregular habits and tempting excitements of life' to deter only the most desperate from seeking refuge within the workhouse.

The shadow of the workhouse loomed over most members of the working class and even some of the middle class. Orphaned families and foundling children as well as women with large families who were suddenly widowed were probably the most common estimates. Delicate children or those suffering from epilepsy or disabilities were also likely to end up in the workhouse, particularly during economic downturn or famine.

The Poor Law system was barely in operation before the catastrophe of the Great Famine hit Ireland. As famine and fever spread the government permitted Poor Law Commissioners to authorise boards to give food to the able-bodied poor for limited periods. The Ulster Guardians, in general, proved to be less willing to grant outdoor relief to the unemployed than their southern counterparts. In July 1847 the Belfast Guardians made it clear that outdoor relief would be granted in only the most extreme cases:

When the workhouse accommodation becomes insufficient, outdoor relief to be afforded to destitute poor persons permanently disabled from labour by old age or bodily or mental infirmity, and who have been resident in the union for not less than the last three years, the relief to be given food only and this cooked and to be issued by relieving officers at suitable depots. Able-bodied persons applying for relief on the grounds of destitution and inability to support them-selves by labour to be relieved within the workhouse only where the means will be provided for keeping them fully employed at stone-breaking, grinding corn or other task work calculated to repay the cost of their maintenance . . .

Various charitable organisations tried to help by establishing soup kitchens in Belfast and feeding as many as 15,000 a day. The Guardians feared that soup kitchens, such as those at Howard Street and York Street, only exasperated the problem by encouraging vagrants to flock to Belfast:

Ejectment, Illustrated London News, *1848.*

It being notorious that a large majority of the poor born in this union have flocked into it from other and distant counties, attracted by the reputation of the local charities, and have thus become the means of importing disease and demoralisation, adding very considerably to the local taxation and threatening to increase it to a still larger amount, it will now become the duty of the ratepayers and inhabitants of the union to discourage the influx of vagrants from other localities . . .

By 1847 almost every person admitted into workhouses was a patient suffering from either dysentery, fever or were in the early stages of disease. In June 1847 the Board of Guardians received a deputation from the Board of Health that urged that some provision should be made for the burial of the poor dying in the town. According to the minutes:

The ground which the Charitable Society have granted for the purpose cannot admit of any fresh burials after 1st July if the present rate of mortality continues. The Shankill burying ground is full; a month more will completely fill that of Friar's Bush. There are no other nor is there any public body in the town having the power to purchase or appropriate ground for the purpose and the Board of Health expressly state that after the period above-mentioned the bodies of the poor must lie unburied unless a burying ground can be provided by the Board of Guardians or the Poor Law Commissioners under the powers of the act for the relief of the poor already passed.

The Guardians were answerable to local ratepayers and were expected to account for all monies spent in the administration of the workhouse. This can be seen in the account book that has survived for Lurgan Board of Guardians. This volume provides a detailed record of the inmates who were admitted to the workhouse during the 1840s. It appears to be the only volume of its kind to have survived in the massive Board of Guardian archive deposited at PRONI and gives invaluable information about the local poor and destitute, sick and elderly, who are not usually found in tithe or valuation records. The following extract demonstrates the calibre of information contained in this one, rather battered volume:

Electoral Division of Maralin 18 Inmates. Week Ending 17 August 1844

Dowey, Mary	6	Healthy	–	March, 15, 1841	
Close, Uriah	8	–	Ballymacateer	Feby, 24, 1884	
Lawther, Anne	35	–	Ballymacateer	October 5, 1843	"
Archer, Anne Jane	10	–	–	"	
McKinley, Margaret	4	–	–	"	
Baxter, Mary	55	–	Balymakeonan	"	
Magra, Mary Anne	25	–	Ballymacmain	Octr. 12, 1843	
McKinley, Anne	67	Insane	–	Decr. 21, 1843	
Hughes, William	38	Paralytic	–	Balymakeonan	"
McAmley, Margaret	35	Healthy	Balymakeeonan	Feby. 22, 1844	
McAmley, Isabella	7	–	–	"	
McAmley, William	3	–	Edenballycoggill	"	
Caves, Thomas	55	Bad leg		May, 2, 1844	

Between November 1846 and March 1847, the number of paupers in Enniskillen workhouse doubled. Numbers reached a peak in May 1847 when it was recorded that 'there are 1,433 paupers in a building designed to house 1,000'. Local newspapers reported the distressing conditions faced by inmates in the neighbouring workhouses. The *Impartial Reporter* recorded events on 4 May 1847 when 351 men, women and children, who had been waiting in the grounds of the workhouse all day as the Guardians met, forced their way inside:

Children appeared to be dying in the act of endeavouring to extract sustenance from the dried up breast of their parents, others more mature in years were propped up by some relative or acquaintance who was fast hastening to a similar state of weakness. The general appearance was truly sickening. An endeavour was made to enter the names when, some fearing they might be excluded, another rush was made and put *hors de combat* the guardians at the board. The horrors of the black hole of Calcutta were endured by them for a time – they rushed to the window and gasped for breath.

As a direct result of the extraordinary circumstances brought about by the Famine, exceptional measures were introduced in Ireland in order to prevent the complete breakdown of the workhouse system. In June 1847 a separate Irish Poor Law Commission was set up and put in charge of further assistance under the Poor Relief (Ireland) Act. The 1847 Act also permitted the Board of Guardians to grant outdoor relief to the aged, infirm and sick poor, and to poor widows with two or more dependant children. The Enniskillen Board of Guardians welcomed the fact that the Poor Law Commissioners had declared that able-bodied paupers were still to go to the workhouse which they felt sure would 'prevent imposition from idle able-bodied persons'. Nevertheless, they were concerned that the granting of outdoor relief would be an ever increasing burden upon the rate payers of the Union.

As a means of reducing the numbers of destitute persons and lessening the burden of the crippling poor rate on the landowners the government gave its wholehearted support to assisted emigration schemes. The Poor Relief Acts of 1838, 1843, 1847 and 1849 empowered the Boards of Guardians to raise such sums 'not exceeding the proceeds of one shilling in the pound' of the annual poor rate to 'assist poor persons who would otherwise have to be accommodated in the workhouse' to emigrate, preferably to the British colonies. The Colonial Land and Emigration Commission was set up in England in 1840, under the control of the British Colonial Office, to organise and supervise emigration from both Britain and Ireland. The availability of emigration was constantly brought to the attention of the Boards of Guardians in circular letters issued by the Poor Law Commissioners. The representative of the Emigration Commission visited every workhouse in Ireland to inspect and select persons for emigration and those chosen were offered a free passage and supplied before departure with clothing and a little money to support themselves on arrival.

During the later part of the nineteenth century the Boards of Guardians played an important role in the administration of local government. In 1872, the Boards of Guardians came under the control of the Local Government Board, which became one of the most important departments of the Irish administration. To its original functions of supervising the Poor Law and the dispensary system, the government added many others including responsibility for public health. From 1856 Boards of Guardians acted as burial boards and from 1865 as sewer authorities for those areas of the counties that were outside the responsibility of the Town Commissioners. The Guardians' powers were further increased by the Public Health Acts of 1874 and 1878 which made the Poor Law Boards rural sanitary authorities giving them power to destroy unsound food, supervise slaughter houses and deal with infectious diseases in hospitals. The Guardians later were made responsible for the supervision of the hospitals set up under the Tuberculosis Prevention (Ireland) Act of 1908 and the Board also became the central authority under the Old Age Pensions Act of 1908.

In 1898, when the Local Government Act was introduced, the power of the Irish Boards of Guardians began its steady decline. This Act confined the duties of the Boards of Guardians to poor relief, while their other functions were taken over by the county councils. By this time the workhouse was the last refuge for the old, the sick and children. The Poor Law system remained largely intact in Northern Ireland until 1948, by which time the health and welfare functions of the Boards of Guardians were transferred to local health authorities and county councils.

Potato dinner, Pictorial Times, *28 February 1846*.

The records

The Poor Law Unions kept a number of different types of records. The National Archive lists fifteen classes: Minute books, Correspondence, Accounts, Statistics, Out-Relief, Workhouse Administration, Workhouse Inmates, Workhouse Infirmary, Boarding Out, Dispensary, Returns of Births and Deaths, Vaccination, Contagious Diseases, Assessment and Miscellaneous. These were then divided into sub-classes, and even this classification does not cover every type of record one might possibly find.

Of all the records, the Registers of Admission and Discharge are the most valuable. Unfortunately, the registers have not survived as well as other Poor Law Union records. Of all the classes, the minute books are probably the best preserved. They contain miscellaneous information about the administration of the Poor Law Unions, and often include details of staff employed by the Poor Law Union.

The surviving records of the twenty-seven Poor Law Unions in the counties of Northern Ireland are held by PRONI as listed below. For details of the records which have survived for each Union, researchers should consult the grey calendars, which are available on the shelves of the Public Search Room.

BG/1	Antrim, County Antrim
BG/2	Armagh, County Armagh
BG/3	Ballycastle, County Antrim
BG/4	Ballymena, County Antrim
BG/5	Ballymoney, County Antrim
BG/6	Banbridge, County Down
BG/7	Belfast, Counties Antrim and Down
BG/8	Castlederg, County Tyrone
BG/9	Clogher, County Tyrone
BG/10	Coleraine, County Londonderry
BG/11	Cookstown, County Tyrone
BG/12	Downpatrick, County Down
BG/13	Dungannon, County Tyrone
BG/14	Enniskillen, County Fermanagh
BG/15	Irvinestown, County Fermanagh
BG/16	Kilkeel, County Down
BG/17	Larne, County Antrim
BG/18	(Newton) Limavady, County Londonderry
BG/19	Lisburn, County Antrim
BG/20	Lisnaskea, County Fermanagh
BG/21	Londonderry, County Londonderry
BG/22	Lurgan, County Armagh
BG/23	Magherafelt, County Londonderry

BG/24   Newry, County Down

BG/25   Newtownards, County Down

BG/26   Omagh, County Tyrone

BG/27   Strabane, County Tyrone

BG/28   Gortin, County Tyrone (united to Omagh *c.* 1870)

It is important to note that most Board of Guardian records are closed for 100 years from the latest date in each volume. As in the rest of the UK, criteria exist for the extended closure (i.e., beyond 30 years) of certain categories of records. The relevant category in relation to the Board of Guardian records is 'documents containing information about individuals, the disclosure of which would cause distress or danger to living persons or their descendants'. Unfortunately for the family historian, most classes of the BG records contain sensitive information relating to the boarding out or fostering of children. The workhouse was the chief residence of unmarried pregnant girls and orphaned or foundling children. Understandably, in a place as small as Northern Ireland, individuals are anxious that such details are not available to the general public.

Chapter 14

LOCAL-GOVERNMENT RECORDS

Corporations

A city or town corporation was a local administrative body formed for the purposes of government by municipal officers. From medieval times, city or town corporations were created by patent held of the Crown. In Ulster, with the exception of Carrickfergus and Downpatrick, corporations were seventeenth-century creations. The corporations in Northern Ireland often performed no function apart from electing Members of Parliament. This was partly due the fact that many of them were little more than villages and partly because some, like Belfast, were dominated by powerful patrons.

A Municipal Reform Act of 1840 abolished the existing corporations, preserving borough councils in just ten places, including Belfast and Londonderry in Northern Ireland. These corporate bodies comprised a mayor, aldermen and councillors: to be eligible for office, candidates were required to be on the burgess roll and possessed of property, real or personal, to the value of £1,000 over and above any debts, or to be the occupier of a house rated for Poor Law purposes at £25 p.a.

Belfast Corporation

Belfast was constituted as a corporate town in 1613. The government of the town was vested by charter in the Lord and Constable of the Castle, the sovereign and burgesses. However, it was the sovereign who was responsible for the day-to-day administration of the town. According to an account of Belfast published in 1823, his principal duties were to hold a court 'for the trial of petty offences, and who is empowered to make different regulations for the administration of public affairs. His authority for regulating the markets, weights, and some other matters of a minor, is also recognised within the borough'. The earliest surviving records of the Corporation were reprinted in R M Young (ed.), *The town book of the Corporation of Belfast, 1613–1816* (Marcus Ward, 1892; recently republished, Belfast, 2008). It is a record of the Corporation's activities, and records the election of sovereigns, the replacement of burgesses and the making of bylaws.

The Linen Hall and operatives, Belfast, Irish Pictures Drawn with Pen and Pencil, *Richard Lovett (1888).*

Belfast Corporation records are located in the Local Authority archive deposited at PRONI. They contain a wide variety of records including wages and salaries books, rent books and rate ledgers. Those of most interest to family historians are as follows:

- 'Borough Rate' Ledgers, 1843–53, LA/7/5BA/1;

- 'Borough Rate' Ledgers Applotment Books, 1843–71, LA/7/5BA/2;

- 'Improvement Rate' Books, 1846–66, LA/7/5BA/3;

- Burial Rate Book, 1868, LA/7/5BA/4;

- Police Rate Books, 1868–71, LA/7/5BA/5;

- General Purposes Rate Book, 1868–71, LA/7/5BA/6;

- Drainage District Rate Book, 1874–1909, LA/7/5BA/7;

- Police, General Purposes, Borough and Special (Malicious Injury) Rate Book, 1881–1902, LA/7/5BA/8;

- Belfast Corporation Market Committee Wages Book, 1847–1946, LA/7/21FA/1–21;

- Town Council Rent Book, 1851–82, LA/7/12G/1.

Many of the rate ledgers listed above contain the names of both the owners of the properties and their tenants.

Other corporations

Armagh, County Armagh

- Corporation records, 1731–1840, Armagh Public Library;
- Extracts from Armagh corporation minute books, 1731–1818, PRONI T/808/14932, 14983, 15318;

Carrickfergus, County Antrim

- Volume of *c.* 90 pages containing information about Carrickfegus corporation, *c.* 1568–*c.* 1689 PRONI D/162/1;
- List of burgesses and freemen of the corporation, n.d. (pre-1706) PRONI D/162/18.

Clogher, County Tyrone

- Extracts from corporation book, 1783–98, PRONI T/1566.

Coleraine, County Londonderrry

- Minute books of the Court of Common Council of the Corporation of Coleraine, 1672–1707, 1707–10, 1792–1840 (original and copies,) PRONI LA/25/2AA/1A–2;
- Box of miscellaneous eighteenth-century papers relating to the Corporation, including a list of members of the Corporation in 1782, PRONI D/668/O/1.

Dungannon, County Tyrone

- Corporate minute books, 1695–1840, PRONI MIC/547/1.

Hillsborough, County Down

- Corporation books, 1740–74, 1773–1841, PRONI D/671/O/1.

Limavady, County Londonderry

- Corporate minute books, 1659–1736, 1736–68, 1771–81, 1781–1808, PRONI D/663/2–5, published as *Records of the Town of Limavady, 1609 to 1808*, edited by E M F-G Boyle (Londonderry 1912; reprinted Limavady, 1989).

Londonderry, County Londonderry

- Minute books of Londonderry Corporation, 1673–1841 (with gaps), PRONI LA/79/2AA/1-11B.

Newtownards, County Down

- Corporate minute book, 1741–75, LA60/2AB/1;
- Borough act book, 1742–75, PRONI T/433/1;
- Minute book of the grand jury of the corporation, 1756–1833, PRONI, LA/60/2AA/1.

Strabane, County Tyrone

- Corporation council minutes, 1755–1812;
- Corporation minutes, accounts and borough court proceedings, 1769–1850;
- Jury book, 1773–1810, PRONI MIC/159/1.

Town Commissioners

The Lighting of Towns (Ireland) Act of 1828, established Town Commissions with responsibility for lighting and cleaning. More were established under the Towns Improvement Act

Carrickfergus Castle, The Scenery and Antiquities of Ireland, *drawn by W H Bartlett (1841).*

(1854), which also gave the Commissions more powers in the areas of cleaning and paving of streets; the prevention of fire; the safeguarding of the community from dangerous buildings; the regulation of traffic and the licensing of hackney carriages. Later acts authorised Town Commissioners to establish and regulate markets, and gave them power to formulate housing schemes.

The Town Commissioners' Minute Books provide a considerable amount of material that will be of interest to genealogists. Lists of names appear for a variety of reasons in minute books and some rate books. Records for Town Commissioners in Northern Ireland are held in the Local Authority archive, PRONI reference LA.

Lists of Town Commissioners also appear in the local newspapers. This can help fill the gaps where the records have not survived, as is the case in the following extract taken from the *Newry Commercial Telegraph*, 11 July 1837. Each of the twenty-one persons named were expected to serve for three years:

1. Dennis Maguire	12. William Blackham
2. Trevor Corry	13. Rowan McNaughten
3. Pat. McParlan	14. Robert Stewart
4. Henry Waring	15. James G. Quin
5. James Spence	16. James Lyle
6. Peter Quinn	17. Patrick Christopher Byrne
7. Richard Liddy	18. Hugh Dalzell
8. George Scott	19. Michael Cunningham
9. Robert Greer	20. William Henry
10. David Gillis	21. Charles O'Hagan
11. Charles Jennings	

Grand Jury

The Grand Jury was appointed yearly by the county High Sheriff and had both judicial and administrative responsibilities. Its judicial function was to preside at the assizes and examine bills of indictment relating to criminal matters. Administrative tasks were undertaken at presentment sessions. These special sessions were most often used for raising money for specific purposes, such as the upkeep and building of roads and bridges and the supervision of workhouses, gaols, fever hospitals and other county institutions. Expenditure was financed through a system of local taxation known as the county cess.

Grand Jury Presentments are the chief records of the county administration prior to 1898. These and Grand Warrants contain information about work ordered to be done by the Grand Jury on roads, bridges and jails and constabulary duties in the counties. They are often arranged barony by barony within the county and useful genealogical information can be obtained by detailed searching of them. They are not indexed. Although frequently printed, different sets contain manuscript amendments and notes according to who owned and used them.

City and Liberties of Londonderry

366 – To Peter McGrath, to keep in repair, for 7 years, from Spring Assizes, 1837, 164 perches of road from Londonderry to Lifford, between Mr. Harvey's and Charles Murphy's, in the townland of Molenan, at 6d. (21) £2 1s 0d.

Securities, John Pinkerton and John Forsythe.

Grand Jury Presentments Summer Assizes, 1839, PRONI LOND/4/1/12.

Also of interest are the lists of Grand Jurors which include the names of qualified jurors, their places of residence and occupations (referred to in the lists as: title, quality, calling or business). The qualification for jury service from 1692 onwards was that jurors had to own property valued at £10 annually. In later acts, substantial leaseholders were also included as jurors.

Grand Jury records for Northern Ireland are held at PRONI. The most useful records are listed below and can be found in the Crown and Peace archive:

County Antrim

- ANT/4: Presentments, 1711–1840;
- LA7/60: Presentments, 1867–95;
- T/1110: Jury lists, 1613–1803;
- T/976–7: Grand Jury lists, 1814–43;
- T/1329: Grand Jury lists for Antrim assizes, 1843–60.

County Armagh

- D/288/112: Presentments, 1790;
- ARM/4/1: Presentments, 1758–1899;
- T/647: Jury Lists, 1735–97.

County Down

- DOW/4/2: Presentments, 1778–1899.

County Fermanagh

- FER/4/1–3: Presentments, 1792–1898.

County Londonderry

- LON/4/1: Presentments, 1788–1899;
- Grand Jury Lists, 1614–1819;
- Book containing the names of the Recorder's Court Grand Jurors of the City and County of Londonderry, 1857–99.

County Tyrone

- TYR/4/1: Presentments, 1799–1897.

County councils

County councils were established in 1899 superseding the Grand Juries and taking on many of the functions held by the Boards of Guardians. By the early part of the twentieth century there was a steady growth in the powers of the county councils as they acquired housing and planning powers. They were responsible for elementary and secondary education. The county councils divided the county into districts for the management by a district committee of public heath, housing, roads and water supply.

The most important records for the local historian are the minutes and other records of the council itself and of its committees and the accounts. Local authority records for Northern Ireland are deposited at PRONI and can be located under the reference LA.

Chapter 15

MILITARY RECORDS

Before the Union with Great Britain in 1801, Ireland had a separate Army with its own organisation and establishment (although the British Army drew heavily on Irish recruits). From 1801, Ireland remained a separate command, and the Irish regiments retained their Irish identity, but the Army was merged with the British Army. Ireland was a popular recruiting area for the British Army over the centuries. Many young men with a taste for adventure or the desire to escape unemployment at home served in various regiments throughout the Empire.

It was customary before the First World War for regiments to recruit primarily within a local district. The market town of Enniskillen, once one of the principal strongholds of the Ulster Plantation, has the unique distinction of giving its name to two of the oldest and most-famous regiments of the British Army: the 27th Foot (known as the Royal Inniskilling Fusiliers) and the Royal Inniskilling Dragoons. The Royal Irish Fusiliers recruited in the counties of Armagh, Louth, Cavan and Monaghan, the Royal Irish Rifles in counties Antrim, Down and Louth. Of course many Irishmen joined English regiments. The National Archives, London, has records for men and women who

Lord Charlemont, painted by Richard Liversay, National Gallery of Ireland, Dublin.

left the services before the end of 1920. It is important that you know when your ancestor was in the forces and the regiment or unit with which they served.

For the nineteenth century the National Archives, London, has several series of records detailing the service of officers and an alphabetical card index to these records is available. The National Archives, London, has correspondence about the sale and purchase of commissions between 1793 and 1871 in series WO 31. This contains a great deal of valuable genealogical information. Records of military commissions and appointments of Irish officers between 1768 and 1877 are in HO 123.

For information on ancestors who served in the rank and file the most useful records available at Kew are the soldiers' documents in series WO 97.

Records relating to the Army in Ireland, 1775–1923, are in WO35. Muster rolls of the Irish militia, 1793–1876, are in WO 13. The Royal Kilmainham Hospital, founded in 1679, acted as a hospital for disabled soldiers (known as in-pensioners) and also distributed money to out-pensioners: there are registers of in- and out-pensioners in the admission books, 1704–1922 (WO 118) and discharge documents, 1783–1822 (WO 119).

Other Irish soldiers and sailors had their pensions paid by the Royal Chelsea Hospital or by Greenwich Hospital. Records of these pensions, 1842–62 and 1882–83, are in WO 22/141–205 and WO 22/209–225. They can be used to trace changes of residence and dates of death. The only separate naval records for Irishmen are of nominations to serve in the Irish Coastguard, 1821–49 (ADM 175/99–100).

For a more complete list see Simon Fowler's, *Tracing Your Army Ancestors* (Pen & Sword Books, 2006) and *Army Service Records of the First World War* (Countryside Books, 2003).

The General Register Office in Belfast has some records relating to service personnel from 1930.

The regimental museums are another useful source of information.

The Royal Irish Fusiliers Museum

The museum is situated in Sovereign's House, a fine Georgian building dating from 1809 and the first house built on Armagh's Mall. It celebrates the history of the Royal Irish Fusiliers, which is closely associated with the city of Armagh. The museum has interpretative displays covering the history of the Regiment and the Armagh, Cavan and Monaghan Militias from 1793 to 1968. There are fine exhibitions of uniforms, trophies, badges and medals. They are proud owners of the VCs won by Robert Morrow and Geoffrey Cather. The archive includes contemporary letters/diaries, battalion war diaries and discharge papers. Also of interest are photograph albums, war diaries and regimental histories. The contact details are:

The Royal Irish Fusiliers Regimental Museum
Sovereign's House
The Mall
Armagh
BT61 9DL
Northern Ireland
Email: mailto:rylirfusilierus@aol.com
Website: www.rirfus-museum.freeserve.co.uk.

The Royal Inniskillen Fusiliers Regimental Museum

The regimental museum is situated in the magnificent setting of Enniskillen Castle, once the medieval stronghold of the Maguires. The museum is housed in the Castle Keep and has displays that span the history of the Regiment from its formation in 1689 up to modern times. The contact details are:

The Castle
Enniskillen
BT74 7HL
County Fermanagh
Northern Ireland

The Regimental Museum of The Royal Ulster Rifles

The Museum (formerly the Royal Irish Rifles) has over 4,000 artefacts on show, including uniforms, trophies, badges and medals, with the VC won by James Byrne. Also of interest are photograph albums, war diaries and library. The contact details are:

Regimental Headquarters
The Royal Irish Rangers
5 Waring Street
Belfast
BT1 2EW

Militia

The militia was a force originally intended for home defence and was a far older institution than the regular Army. Although service in the regular Army was voluntary for much of its history, men were obliged to serve in the part-time militia, if they were selected in a local ballot. Catholics only began to enter the lowest ranks late in the eighteenth century.

Local constables were empowered to draw up lists of all the able-bodied men in their area. A ballot was then held to decide which of these men were to be called upon to serve or else pay for a replacement. Peers, clergymen, articled clerks, apprentices and those who had served previously were among those who were exempt. Also any man selected by the ballot to serve could be excused service if he could provide a suitable substitute. Volunteers frequently prevented the raising of men by compulsion. The local gentry who provided the militia high command used their considerable influence to keep their militia regiments well supplied by volunteer recruits.

In 1793 the revolutionary government of France declared war on Great Britain and the Irish militia regiments were reorganised to meet the threat posed by both France and the United Irishmen. These regiments were embodied more or less continuously until the defeat of Napoleon in 1815. For the most part they were employed on garrison duty in various parts of Ireland and provided drafts of volunteers to the regular Army. They also played an important role during the 1798 Rebellion in Ireland.

All the militia regiments were re-embodied in 1855 when war broke out in the Crimea. Once again the militia regiments were generally used for garrison duties which freed the regular Army for duty in the Crimea. In 1881, as part of a general reorganisation of the Army, all militia regiments were reclassified as battalions of regular Army regiments but retained their militia status. The last period of embodiment for these regiments was the Boer War (1899–1902). During the First World War they were used for recruitment and training.

Militia muster rolls for Ireland between 1793 and 1876 are held by the National Archives, London,

Roaring Meg, Irish Pictures Drawn with Pen and Pencil, *Richard Lovett (1888).*

reference WO 13. In the same series are musters of volunteers, 1797–1814 and 1873–78. They are arranged by county and list alphabetically men's names, their ages and parish. Irish militia records are also held at the following locations:

Belfast

- List of Belfast Militia Company, May 1692, Trinity College, Ms 1178;

- Returns of Belfast Militia, May, 1692, Ulster Museum, Acc. 145–1950.

County Antrim

- Payments to the Antrim Militia, January 1691; list of officers of Antrim Militia, May 1692, Trinity College Ms 1178;

- Lists of Antrim Militia Corps, 1760, Dublin Royal Irish Academy, Ms 24k.19;

- Militia Officers, 1761, PRONI T/808/15235;

- Militia Pay Lists and Muster Rolls, 1799–1800, PRONI T/1115/1A & B.

County Armagh

- Militia Officers, 1761, T/808/15235;

- Militia Lists by parish in the barony of O'Neil land west, 1793–95, PRONI D/1928/Y/1;

- Militia Pay Lists and Muster Rolls, 1799–1800, PRONI T/1115/2A-C;

- List of Officers of Armagh Militia, 1808, PRONI T/561;

- Muster Rolls, Armagh Militia, 1793–97, PRONI D/183.

County Down

- Militia Officers, 1761, PRONI T/808/15235;

- Oath and List of Names of Ballyculter Supplementary Corps, 1798, PRONI T/1023/153.

County Fermanagh

- Notebooks containing list of Fermanagh Militia, April 1708, NLI Ms 2696;

- Militia Officers, 1761, PRONI T/808/15235;

- Militia Pay Lists and Muster Rolls, 1794–99, PRONI T/1115/5A-C.

County Londonderry

- Militia Officers, 1761, PRONI T/808/15235, GO 680.

County Tyrone

- Militia Officers, 1761, PRONI T/808/15235;

- Pay Roll of the Aghnahoe Infantry, 1829–32, PRONI D/1927.

Yeomanry

The yeomanry were formed in September 1796 under the threat of imminent invasion from France. The local gentry and magistrates throughout Ireland were empowered to raise infantry companies and cavalry troops in order to maintain a military presence in the absence of troops and militia called upon to intercept any invasion. The government paid, clothed and armed this volunteer force and their main function was to free the regular Army and militia from their local peacekeeping activities. Service was usually two days per week and members were expected to turn out during emergencies. Despite the intentions of the government, it became a largely Protestant force in Ulster and after the Union of 1800 with Great Britain it remained a powerful symbol of Protestant determination to retain control of law and order in the north. The formation of the County Constabulary and a decade later the Irish Constabulary removed the need for such as peacekeeping force but the Yeomanry lingered on until it was officially disbanded in 1834.

The names of those local grandees who commanded local militia and yeomany regiments were published during the eighteenth and nineteenth centuries. These will be available at major libraries such as the Linen Hall Library and Central Library in Belfast or the local Irish History Libraries supported by the Education and Library Boards. On the shelves of the Linen Hall Library, for example, there are more than 200 volumes of Army, Navy and militia lists giving local and national information.

Muster books for the Yeomanry are held at Kew (WO 13/4059–4159). They are arranged by county and then by corps. They name the men and give their dates of service. Sadly they are only available from 1823 to 1834.

Various repositories in Ireland also hold yeomanry lists and related material. The most important are given below.

County Antrim

• List of yeomanry corps, 1804, RAI Ms 24k.19.

County Armagh

• Crowhill Yeomanry pay list, c. 1820, PRONI T/2701;
• Ardress Yeomanry Book, c. 1796, PRONI D/296;
• Churchill Yeomanry Book, c. 1796, PRONI D/321/1.

County Down

• Killyleagh Yeomanry List, 1798, PRONI D/303;
• Mourne Yeomanry Lists, 1824, PRONI T/991.

County Fermanagh

• Yeomanry Muster Rolls, 1797–1804, PRONI T/808/15244.

County Londonderry

• Yeomanry Muster Rolls, 1797–1804, PRONI T/1021/3.

General

- Extracts of Regular Army Muster Rolls, 1741–80, PRONI T/808/15196.

Volunteers

The Volunteers were a part-time military force raised locally in companies and battalions during 1778–80. Members were drawn mainly from the Protestant middle classes and officers from the local gentry and aristocracy. Shortly after its formation the Volunteers adopted a more overtly political role as radical politicians took leading positions in the force. By 1782 there were 40,000 enlisted in the Volunteers, half of them in Ulster. Strongly influenced by American ideas, though loyal to the Crown, the Volunteers demanded greater legislative freedom for the Dublin Parliament. In 1782 the Volunteers played a major role in forcing the British government to concede the independence of the Irish Parliament. They then campaigned for the reform of the legislature itself and began to falter in 1784 as a result of the divisions caused by the question of Catholic Emancipation. Although they lost their national importance, they continued to exist at a local level. Enthusiasm for Volunteering did recover briefly after 1789 with the excitement caused by the French Revolution. In 1793, however, the Gunpowder Act, prohibiting the import of arms, and the Convention Act, which declared illegal all assemblies for the purpose of soliciting a change in the law that claimed the status of a representative body, effectively ended Volunteering.

Muster rolls for Volunteer regiments, 1797–1814 and 1873–78, are held by the National Archives, London, reference WO 13. They are arranged by county and list alphabetically men's names, their ages and parish.

The following records are also of interest:

- Minute book of Rathfriland Volunteers, 1775, Ulster Museum Acc.571, 603–1914;

- Minute book for the Men of Mourne Volunteer Corps, 1778–1792, PRONI T/1317; Ulster Museum Acc.19–1947;

- Minute book of the first and second Volunteer companies of Newtownards, April and May 1787, PRONI, D/3030;

- Minute books of Newry Ist Volunteer Company, 1778–93, PRONI T/3202;

Volunteers,
1782, *painting by
John Carey,
Lisburn Museum.*

- Minute book of Newry [2nd?] Volunteer Company, 1778–87, PRONI, T/3202;

- List of Antrim Volunteer Corps, 1780–84, RIA Ms 24k.19;

- Copy of Volunteer order, County Down, with extract of Volunteer Muster Roll, 1782, PRONI, T/441.

For more information on Stuart Ireland see Charles Dalton, *Irish Army Lists 1661–1685* (London, 1907).

Chapter 16

ELECTORAL RECORDS

Voters, poll and freeholders' records

Until the eighteenth century elections were held infrequently. Before 1768 there was no law limiting the duration of Irish parliaments and nothing to compel the government to hold a general election except the death of the reigning monarch. The Octennial Act of 1768 provided that a general election should be held at least every eight years. Nevertheless, until the nineteenth century very few elections were contested, and parliamentary representation remained firmly in the hands of a small number of powerful landed families. The extension of the franchise changed this, and by the beginning of the twentieth century the landed classes had to a large extent withdrawn from electoral politics, particularly at representative level.

Before the late nineteenth century the qualification for voting was generally linked to the tenure of land and only a small minority of men had the right to vote. In Ireland, between 1727 and 1793 only Protestants with a freehold worth at least 40s per year had a vote. From 1793 to 1829 both Protestants and Roman Catholics with 40s freeholds had votes, although a Catholic was still unable to become a Member of Parliament. The 40s freehold was property worth 40s a year above the rent, and either owned outright or leased on certain specific terms. Many important and indeed prominent people had no vote because they leased their property on the wrong terms.

One distinctive feature of the county franchise in Ireland was that from 1728 onwards voters had to conform to an increasingly tight system of registration, designed to prevent the creation of fictitious freeholders. This was important because the more 40s freeholders a landlord had on his land, the greater his influence during an election. In 1828, Daniel O'Connell, who led the fight for Catholic Emancipation, won a by-election in County Clare. The fight for the right to sit in Parliament had gained unparalleled support throughout the country and resulted in the Catholic

Relief Act of 1829. Catholics were now allowed to sit in Parliament and to hold government posts, except those of Lord Chancellor, Lord Lieutenant and Regent. However, at the same time as the Relief Act, the qualification for the vote was changed from 40s to £10. This reduced the electorate from 216,000 to 37,000.

The Reform Act of 1832, which although it retained the £10 franchise, admitted certain categories of leaseholder and raised the county electorate to around 60,000. The Irish Franchise Act of 1850 set the county franchise at £12 with the result that the Irish electorate rose from 45,000 to 164,000. The majority of these county electors were farmers and were fairly well-to-do. During these periods of changes in the franchise, lists of those entitled to vote appeared in the local newspapers. These lists are divided by barony and include voters' names and the townland in which they were resident. However, it is important to remember that those entitled to vote only formed a small percentage of the local population. By 1881 the vote in Ireland was limited to 18 per cent of the adult male population. By 1884 the majority of male householders over 21 were entitled to vote. Women did not obtain the vote in general elections until 1918 and even then it was limited to those over 30 who were householders or the wives of householders. It was as late as 1928 that the vote was granted to women over 21.

Poll books

Poll books are the books in which are recorded the votes cast at parliamentary elections. They contain the name and address of the voter and often the address of the 'Freehold' which entitled the voter to his vote. These records predate 1868, the last election before the Ballot Act, which established secret voting. This enabled tenant farmers to register their votes without having to take account of the political views of their landlord. This

An Irish school master from 'Sketches of Irish Life', Illustrated London News, *24 January–21 February 1857.*

had an immediate impact in Ireland and enabled a strong Irish Home Rule party to be formed at Westminster.

Electoral registers and voters' lists

The Parliamentary Reform Act of 1832 required the publication on a parish basis of lists of persons eligible to vote. As the franchise was gradually extended, so the lists have become more comprehensive. Since 1928 (when the age that women were allowed to vote was lowered to 21) they list the names and addresses of all adults who have registered. Copies may be seen at county record offices and public libraries. PRONI, the NLI and NAI have extensive collections of electoral registers, although it is in no sense complete. After 1880 voters' lists are to be found in the Crown and Peace Records for the counties. PRONI has recently digitised about 5,500 sheets from pre-1840 registers and poll books. These can be searched online and images of the original records viewed. See: www.proni.gov.uk/freeholders/intro.asp.

The most generally useful poll books and freeholders' registers held in PRONI are:

County Antrim

- D/1364/1/1: 'Deputy Court Cheque Book', poll book, 1776.

County Armagh

- T/808/14936: poll book, 1753;

- T/808/14949: objections to voters, 1753;

- ARM 5/2/1–17: freeholders' lists, 1813 to 1832;

- T/808/14934: freeholders' registers, 1830 to 1839;

- T/808/14961: freeholders' list, 1839;

- T/808/14927: voters' list, 1851;

- D/1928/F/1–103: freeholders' registers, early eighteenth century to 1830.

County Down

- DOW/5/3/1&2: registers of freeholders, 1777; 1780–95;
- D/654/A3/1B: 'Deputy Court Cheque Book' freeholders' register, 1789;
- T/393/1: freeholders' list (Lecale Barony only), *c.* 1790;
- D/654/A3/1: freeholders' registers, 1813 to 1821; 1824;
- T/761/19&20: freeholders' lists, *c.* 1830;
- D/671/02/5–6: poll book, County Down (Part of), 1852;
- D/671/02/7–8: poll book, County Down (Part of), 1857.

County Fermanagh

- T/808/15063: poll book, 1747–63;
- T/1385: poll book, 1788;
- T/543: poll book, 1788;
- T/808/15075: poll book, 1788;
- D/1096/90: freeholders' registers, 1796 to 1802.

County Londonderry

- T/2123: freeholders' registers (names A to L only), *c.* 1813;
- T/1048/1–4: City of Londonderry voters' list, 1832;
- D/1935/6: City of Londonderry voters' list, 1868;
- D/834/1: freeholders' register, City and County of Londonderry, *c.* 1840;

County Tyrone

- TYR/5/3/1: freeholders' list (Dungannon Barony only), 1795–98.

County Belfast

- D/2472: poll book for Belfast, 1832 to 1837;
- BELF/5/1/1/1–2: register of electors, Belfast, 1855 and 1876.

Chapter 17

LAW AND ORDER

Policing

Despite a series of Acts of Parliament passed during the eighteenth century, the Irish police force at the time of the Act of Union of 1800 was still composed only of small groups of sub-constables. These part-time policemen, appointed by the Grand Juries, were few in number and poorly paid out of the county funds. In 1787, an attempt was made to provide a police force in Ireland. Known as 'Barnies', these policemen quickly proved inadequate for the suppression of disturbances. Sir Robert Peel made another attempt in 1814 with the creation of the Peace Preservation Force, soon dubbed 'Peelers'. They could be called upon by the Lord Lieutenant for use in a district that had been 'proclaimed' as a disturbed area. This force proved inadequate and in 1822 the County Constabulary was established. From 1822 there were two police forces in Ireland: the Peace Preservation Force, which operated in proclaimed districts, and the County Constabulary, which worked to maintain law and order throughout the rest of the country.

The passage of the Irish (Constabulary (Ireland)) Act 1836 finally brought a single, unified force into being. Power to appoint and discharge members of the force, to make rules and to fix salaries was vested in the Lord Lieutenant of Ireland. The Irish Constabulary was responsible for the preservation of law and order throughout the country with the exception of Dublin. The Irish capital retained its own police, the Dublin Metropolitan Police, which had been formed in 1786. Members of the force, who were mainly Catholic, were recruited from among the tenant-farmer class and were removed to distant stations. The force was unpopular in many areas because it was used to assist at evictions and because it supplied Dublin Castle with most of its intelligence information.

The Royal Irish Constabulary was disbanded on 30 August 1922. Pensions continued to be paid by the Paymaster General in London, and the service records of members of the force passed to the Home Office.

PRONI has microfilmed forty-four volumes of registers of service of members of the RIC, 1816–1922. The entries are arranged numerically by service number and give full name, age, height, religious affiliation, native county, trade or calling, marital status, native county of wife, date of appointment, counties in which the man served, length of service, etc. (ref MIC/454).

Also of interest is a register of householders kept by the RIC for the sub-districts of Knocknacarry and Cushendall, 1801–1901 (T/3507). This volume contains a great deal of genealogical material including the names of individuals who are listed as 'gone to America', June 1881.

Records of pensions and allowances made to officers and their widows and children are also held by the National Archives, London, reference, PMG 48. The NA leaflet 'Records of the Royal Irish Constabulary (Domestic Records Information 54)' describes these records in more detail. It can be downloaded from their website at: www.nationalarchives.gov. uk/catalogue/rdleaflet.asp?sLeafletID=244&j=1.

Also of interest is the report of the Belfast Special Constables of nightly watch transactions. This consists of two volumes, 1812–16, and includes an index of all personal names; it is available in transcript form in the relevant calendar in the Search Room at PRONI.

Extract from report of Belfast Special Constabulary, 16 May 1812

Resolved that a nightly watch be appointed for the protection of this town consisting of four constables appointed from the inhabitants and a military guard under their direction to continue for twelve months from this day.

Resolved that two gentlemen from each street be appointed to take down the names of such gentlemen as are capable and willing to act as constables. That the following gentlemen be appointed for that purpose:

Donegall Place and Square	William Clark and William Batt
North Street	Hugh Wilson, James Luke
Donegall Street	Arthur Crawford, William Johnston
Waring Street	Dr Tennent, John Whittle
High Street, Bridge Street to the Quay	William Davison, Mr Gardner
Bridge Street to the Bank Buildings	James McAdam, Dr Bigger
Bridge Street	Mr Black, George Lepper

Rosemary Lane	James Blair, Hugh Johnson
Hercules Lane	George Black, F. Taggart
Castle Street	John McCammon, John Barnett
Ann Street	Campbell Graham, Robert Telfair
Arthur Street	Henry Rowan, William Tucker
Smithfield	A. Bayley, C. Hudson

The courts

For local crime the records of the petty sessions courts, which in most cases survive from the mid-nineteenth century, are useful. More serious crime was dealt with at the assize courts, and though many of the nineteenth-century records were destroyed in 1922 some isolated material has survived.

Shankill Road, RIC barracks after the attack on it in June 1886, Welsh Collection, Ulster Museum.

Crown and Peace records

Before the partition of Ireland, a Clerk of the Crown and Peace in each county maintained the records of the County Court (Court of Quarter Sessions) as well as the records of the Assizes. PRONI has Crown and Peace records dating mostly from the last quarter of the nineteenth century. Among the many classes are Affidavits, Appeals, Civil Bill Books, Convictions, Crown Files at Assizes, Voters' Lists and Registers. All of these contain information on ancestors who were involved in the administration of the legal system, such as local police officers, solicitors and officers of the court as well as those who had fallen foul of the law. The Crown Books contain the names of the Grand Jury, a Calendar of Prisoners, the names of the defendants, witnesses and court officials.

The Crown Books deal with crimes ranging from larceny to assault. Seasonal crimes are also well represented, such as the case of Anne Reilly (also called Anne Fitzpatrick) who appeared before the Newtownbutler Court in December 1877 being charged that she 'did steal take and carry away one domestic fowl to wit a goose of the value of 2/- of the goods of one Robert Maginess against peace'. She was sentenced to one calendar month imprisonment without hard labour.

Also with the Crown and Peace archive are spirit licence registers. These contain the name and address of the trader and of the owner of the premises. The Criminal Injury Books, which give details of individual claims for damages, include the name and address of applicant, solicitors, police officers and witnesses. The claims relate to such matters as the destruction of a building or crops by fire or the breaking of a plate-glass window in a local shop. The applicant claimed damages from the local County Council and if these were awarded they were levied off the relevant townland or electoral division.

One of the most unusual collections to be found within the Crown and Peace archive is the registers of trees. By the end of the seventeenth century a great deal of Ireland's natural woodland had been cut down and timber was beginning to be in short supply. The provisions of the 1765 Act, which stated that on the expiration of his lease, a tenant could claim for the trees he planted, or their value, provided he had lodged a certificate of the trees planted with the clerk of the peace for the county, resulted in the registers of trees that have survived for various counties in Northern Ireland. The registrations were recorded at the quarter sessions and published in the *Dublin Gazette*. Subsequently this information was entered in the ledger entitled Register of Trees in which, depending on the diligence of the justice of the peace, the original affidavits were copied out in full or summarised. This information can be of use to genealogists interested in a particular family that had long-established roots in a particular townland or county. The following ledgers and affidavits are in PRONI.

County Antrim

- Register of Trees, 1841 to 1901. The affidavits are chronologically arranged according to date of registration;

- There is also an affidavit for 1871, ANT/7/6/1;
- Register of Trees for Carrickfergus, 1838, ANT/7/6/2.

County Armagh

- Register of Trees for 1916, ARM/7/6/1.

County Down

- Register of Trees, 1769–99, DOW/7/3/2/1;
- Register of Trees, 1800–22, DOW7/3/2/2;
- Register of Trees, 1823–60, DOW/7/3/2/3.

County Fermanagh

- Three affidavits for the years 1896, 1901, FER/7/3/1.

County Londonderry

- Register of Trees, 1773–1894. Entries arranged alphabetically according to place names, names of tenants, dates of registrations, numbers of trees and species of trees given, LOND/7/7/1;
- A bundle of affidavits covering the years 1834 to 1911, LOND/7/7/2.

County Tyrone

- Register of Trees, 1831–36, TYR/7/3/1;
- Register of Trees, 1835–1916, TYR/7/3/2.

Chapter 18

EMIGRATION

During the eighteenth century more than ¼ million Scotch-Irish Presbyterian settlers left Ireland in search of religious freedom and unoccupied land in the colonies of North America. Braving the hazards of the Atlantic in fragile wooden ships, they landed at Pennsylvania, Delaware, South Carolina and New York, before leading the trek westward to the American frontiers. Fighting native Indian tribes, British colonial forces and the extremes of weather and landscape they helped forge a new nation. President Theodore Roosevelt paid these early settlers a glowing tribute in his book *Episodes from the Winning of the West*: 'They were a bold and hardy people who pushed past the settled regions of America and plunged into the wilderness as the leaders of the white advance. The Irish Presbyterians were the first and last set of immigrants to do all this: all the others have merely followed in the wake of their predecessors'.

To those early emigrants, America was seen as a land where freedom of religion was guaranteed. This first great wave of emigration began in earnest in 1718. In the summer of that year James McGregor, Dissenting Minister of the Aghadowey congregation in County Londonderry, announced to his congregation in the meeting house in June 1718 the first mass emigration of Scots-Irish to the New World: 'Brethren, let us depart for God has appointed a new country for us to dwell in. It is called New England. Let us be free of these Pharaohs, these rackers of rents and screwers of tithes and let us go into the land of Canaan. We are the Lord's ain people and he shall divide the ocean before us.'

Sometimes an enterprising landlord would encourage his tenants to emigrate. Arthur Dobbs from Carrickfergus in County Antrim purchased with Colonel John Selwyn 400,000 acres of land in the south-east of North Carolina in 1745. He was active in seeking out settlers for his land – even offering to pay their passage money – because the terms of his grant laid down that any land on which fewer than one white settler for every

200 acres had been planted by 1755 would revert to the Crown. In 1771, when the leases expired on the large estate of the Marquis of Donegall in County Antrim the rents were raised to such an extent that many tenants could not pay and were subsequently evicted form their farms. During the next three years nearly a hundred vessels sailed from the ports in Ulster.

The American colonies especially attracted those who were eager to

improve their prospects – younger sons in particular. The appeal of America was avidly recounted in letters home to friends and relatives. On 12 May 1785, John Dunlop, a committed patriot who was responsible for the printing of the Declaration of Independence, wrote to his bother-in-law in Strabane, County Tyrone, extolling the advantages of the New World: 'People with a family advanced in life find great difficulties in emigration, but the young men of Ireland who wish to be free and happy should leave it and come hear as quick as possible. There is no place in the world where a man meets so rich a reward for good conduct and industry as in America.' By the time of his death in 1812, Dunlop had acquired 98,000 acres in Kentucky and Virginia.

Emigrants' departure, Illustrated London News, *1850.*

It was cheaper to travel to Quebec from the port of Londonderry than to go from Belfast or Liverpool to Boston or New York. The voyage was also usually shorter. The first large-scale settlement of Upper Canada came when Loyalists – many of them Scots-Irish – fled from the USA during the American War of Independence. A second wave of immigration, coming directly from Ulster, consisted of disbanded soldiers and small farmers hit by the agricultural slump that followed the Napoleonic Wars. Canadian territory in the post-Napoleonic Wars era was attractive in that there was less competition for it than for land on the eastern seaboard of the United States. One visitor to Canada in the early part of the nineteenth century commented that:

from the number of Irish and Scotch who have found their way into Canada by a detour through the States, for few or none have come direct, and from the satisfaction they express with their situation and prospects, one might be led to consider this country as the natural receptacle for our superabundant population. But the northern Irish only, chiefly from the counties of Down, Antrim, Londonderry, Tyrone and Donegal, have as yet, settled in the province . . .

By comparison with the immense emigration to America and Canada during the Great Famine, emigration to Australia was generally a trickle until the discovery of gold in 1851. Nearly 100,000 Irish emigrants came during the 1850s, more than double the rate of the previous decade and a half. A similar flood of emigrants occurred during the 1860s as a result of the Civil War in America. Those emigrants who arranged their travel to Australia were generally better off than those who left Ireland for North America. Few Irish emigrants could afford the full fare of about £17. Australia, therefore, attracted a significant proportion of emigrants with the resources to set themselves up in business or on the land in the expanding agricultural hinterland of the coastal settlements.

There were, however, government-assisted schemes such as the emigration of workhouse inmates to Australia. Labour had become extremely scarce in Australia around the time of the Famine in Ireland and the colonists in New South Wales and Western Australia pressed the Colonial Office to secure more settlers. Arrangements were made with the Colonial Land and Emigration Commissioners for a scheme of assisted emigration and the first 5,000 adults were sent in 1847. At the same time every Australian colony offered financial encouragement for emigration. These ranged from land guarantees to free passages.

Public Record Office of Northern Ireland, Belfast

PRONI has a wide range of records relating to emigration. Letters written from emigrants to their relatives in Ulster form the most substantial part of these emigration records. Emigrant letters can be found in many of the private collections deposited at PRONI. The earliest Ulster letter relating to emigration, which is deposited in PRONI, dates from 1758 and was written by David Lindsey to his cousin Thomas Fleming in Pennylvania. The letter illustrates the attraction of cheap land across the Atlantic and the pressure on the land system at home. Lindsey writes:

The good bargins of your land in that country doe greatly encourage me to 'pluck up my spirits' and make redie for the journey, for we are now oppressed with our lands at 8s. per acre and other improvements, cutting our land in two-acre pasts and quicking, and only two years for doing it all -yea, we cannot stand more.

The following passengers lists are held by PRONI and relate largely to destinations in the USA:

- List of passengers from Warrenpoint and Newry to Philadelphia and New York, 1791–92, T/711/1;

- Passenger lists – Philadelphia, 1800–82, MIC/333/1;

- Passenger lists – Baltimore, 1890–92, MIC/333/2;

- Passenger lists – Boston, 1871–91, MIC/333/3;

- Passenger lists – New York, 1826–27, 1840–42 and 1850–52, MIC/333/4;

- Passengers from various origins arriving mainly in New York, 1802–14, T/1011;

- Passenger lists from Belfast, Cork, Limerick, Londonderry, Newry, Sligo, Warrenpoint to USA, 1803–6, T/3262;

- Passenger lists from Ireland to America, 1804–6 (index available in Deputy Keeper's Report, 1929), T/521/1;

- Passenger books of J & J Cooke, Shipping Agents. Sailings from Londonderry to Philadelphia, Quebec, St John's, New Brunswick, 1847–71, D/2892/1/1–14 (see also MIC/13);

- List of names of petitioners for naturalisation, Laurens County, South Carolina, 1806–25, T/3538;

- Typescript list of passengers to America from County Londonderry, 1815–16, T/2964;

- List of passengers and crew giving age and occupation of people emigrating from Belfast, Cork, Limerick, Londonderry, Newry, Sligo and Warrenpoint, 1805–6, MIC/303.

The Ordnance Survey compilers also recorded the names, ages, religion and townland addresses of emigrants for many parishes in Counties Antrim and Londonderry for a few years during the period 1833–39. Again, Canada and the USA were the major destinations of these emigrants. These two sources have now been indexed and published by the Genealogical Publishing Company of Baltimore.

The following passenger lists are of particular interest to researchers interested in emigration to Canada:

- Three volumes of passenger lists, February 1847–49, February 1850–August 1857, March 1858–July 1867, of J & J Cooke, Shipping Agents, Londonderry. The Canadian destinations are Quebec and St John's, New Brunswick, with details also being given for Philadelphia and New Orleans. D/2892/1/1–3;

- Typed transcripts, compiled in 1984, of notices that appeared in Canadian local newspapers, mostly the *New Brunswick Courier*, 1830–46, and the *Toronto Irish Canadian*, 1869. The notices include queries as to the whereabouts of various persons who had emigrated from Ulster to Canada and the USA. D/3000/82;

- Passenger list, 11 May 1847, issued by A C Buchanan, Chief Agent for Emigration at Quebec, giving the date of sailing, the names of the ships involved, their point of departure and the number of passengers carried. T/3168;

- For details of the early migration from Ulster to Australia see the Crown and Peace Presentment Books for Counties Antrim and Down. ANT/2/2A/1 and DOW/2.

The following records are of particular importance to those interested in making a connection with Australia:

- Passenger list, 1840, Victoria Australia, T/3036;

- Register of Girls' Friendly Society – sponsored emigrants from various counties in Ireland, 1890–1921, D/648/9;

- Indexes to births, deaths and marriages in New South Wales, Australia, 1787–1899, M.F.4;

- In all more than 4,000 orphans were sent to Australia from workhouses in Ireland. The names of those selected from Ulster workhouses are given in the minute books. Further details of their background can be obtained by consulting the admission registers. See the records of the Boards of Guardians, B.G.;

- A more unusual source is the files of the Tuberculosis Authority in the period just after the war. This archive contains two files (1948–57) relating to the X-raying of emigrants who applied for the assisted passage schemes that were on offer to the USA, Australia or New Zealand, TBA 6/5/3–4.

Life in the Bush, *Hutton Picture Library.*

There are many references to parishioners and members of congregations who emigrated to various parts of the world in Church records. These are most commonly found in Presbyterian Church records due to the long-standing association of that Church with emigration. The notations are often found in communion rolls or communicants' rolls and include the date of the emigrants' departure and which members of the family left at that time. The Circuit Schedule Books of Methodist churches record numbers of emigrants from their midst, and occasionally the emigrants are named.

The easiest way to locate emigration records is to search PRONI's Catalogue, containing over 1 million entries, which is now available online for searching and browsing at: www.proni.gov.uk/index.htm.

Ulster American Folk Park

The Ulster American Folk Park's Irish Emigration Database is a computerised collection of primary source documents on Irish emigration to North America (USA and Canada) in the eighteenth and nineteenth centuries. It contains a variety of original material including emigrant letters, newspaper articles, shipping advertisements, shipping news, passenger lists, official government reports, family papers, births, deaths and marriages and extracts from books and periodicals. The project is ongoing and documents are being added on a regular basis. It is a vital research resource for historians, teachers, students and genealogists with interests relating to Irish emigration to North America.

Currently the Irish Emigration Database is available through the Centre for Migration Studies, the Public Records Office Northern Ireland and in Northern Ireland libraries through the Local Studies Departments and public-access terminals in the branch libraries.

Chapter 19

MISCELLANEOUS COLLECTIONS

Solicitors' collections

Solicitors' records are an invaluable source for family historians as they include title deeds, testamentary papers, copy wills, rentals, valuations, etc. Since its foundation the Public Record Office of Northern Ireland has been collecting papers from solicitors' offices in all parts of the Province. Not only do such collections provide numerous copies of destroyed Irish public records, but they provide a wide range of original material that will prove invaluable once the researcher has traced his ancestor to a particular locality.

PRONI holds records of more than 140 Northern Ireland solicitors' practices. These include the records of L'Estrange & Brett, Belfast, which is the most important in the east of the Province. This archive consists of more than 150,000 documents relating to a wide variety of businesses ranging from distillers to the various railway companies operating from Belfast. Most records concern legal disputes or bankruptcy and include title deeds, accounts and related correspondence. The linen industry is well represented with records of the Belfast Flaxspinning and Weaving Company; Acheson Harden Ltd, linen manufacturer; Belfast Flax and Jute Company; and the Northern Spinning & Weaving Company. Also represented are J & J McConnell Ltd and Dunville & Company, distillers; Travers and Company, engineers; W A Ross and Sons Ltd, ironfounders (D/1326). The legal papers of many Belfast families are well represented (D/1905).

The archive of Wilson & Simms, Strabane, has a similar importance west of the Bann. Consisting of more than 20,000 documents, these include a number of landed estate papers in County Donegal, notably those belonging to the Hayes family and the Adair family. Also included are the records of local firms, such as the Longvale Brick and Lime Works Ltd, whose records contain cottiers' rent books and workmen's wages books (D/2298).

In order to find out if the records of a particular firm of solicitors has been deposited at PRONI you can search PRONI's eCatalogue online at: www.proni.gov.uk/.

Business records

Belfast, for much of its history, was dominated by businessmen, merchants and manufacturers. The prosperity of the cotton and linen industries and the rapid growth of trade ensured that Belfast was to become the fastest growing city in the county during the nineteenth century. During the first thirty years of the nineteenth century the cotton and linen industries helped transform Belfast from a small town into a major industrial city. Mr and Mrs Hall, when they visited Belfast during 1840, noted: 'As may be expected, society in Belfast is almost exclusively of a "commercial

Harland and Wolff shipyard with Titanic *in the background, c. 1911, Welsh Collection, Ulster Museum.*

character". There are few resident gentry, that is to say, gentry independent of commerce in the town, although many reside in the immediate neighbourhood.'

Outside Belfast, north-eastern Northern Ireland was the most heavily industrialised region of Ireland. Trade and manufacturing across the Province was largely focused on the linen industry. The main industrialised towns in the county were Newry, Newtownards, Banbridge, Downpatrick and Comber, Lurgan and Portadown. But factories were by no means confined to the towns. There were no less than 6 weaving factories, 2 immense thread mills, 6 bleacheries and 2 beetling mills along the River Bann between Banbridge and Gilford in 1888. Throughout the nineteenth century great factories were established in most of the major towns but handloom weavers working in their own cottages were still counted in their thousands throughout the county until the turn of the century.

PRONI has probably the largest collections of business records in the British Isles. Among them can be found the names of the records that have made Ulster famous throughout the world for linen, ships and engineering. The records themselves represent a wide cross-section of the business life of the Province ranging from the records of Harland and Wolff – builders of the *Titanic* – to the local corner shop. They can be studied alongside related classes of archives deposited by employers, trade unions, public utilities, solicitors, banks and government departments. The lists of employed given in the wages books are the most useful source for family historians.

The most extensive holdings of business records relate to the linen industry: more than 250 companies are represented. These date from the eighteenth century, when spinning and weaving were domestic in character and new methods of bleaching were being devised by the Ulster bleachers. They cover the whole range of business activity, from technical production and employment aspects to marketing on a worldwide scale.

In order to find out if the records of a particular business or company have been deposited at PRONI you can search PRONI's eCatalogue online at: www.proni.gov.uk/.

Orange Order records

Towards the end of the eighteenth century there is ample evidence to show that there was a breakdown in law and order in many parts of Ulster, particularly in counties Armagh and Down. The troubles of the 1780s and 1790s were caused by the increasingly subdivided land among Catholic and Protestant tenants and to the jealousy of Protestants over the increasing entry of Catholics into commercial linen manufacture, which had earlier been dominated by Protestants. Soon the faction fighting that was endemic in rural society assumed a sectarian character. In 1785 an organisation known as the 'Protestant Boys', but more often as the 'Peep-o-Day Boys' because it was at dawn that its members took to appearing at the houses of Catholics and terrorising their occupants into abandoning their smallholdings, began to make its appearance in the North. Local Catholics formed their own organisation called the Defenders and in many parts of Ulster their aims became more militant as they were influenced by events in France brought about by the Revolution there. In September 1795 Defenders assembled at Loughgall at the crossroads known as The Diamond to face the Peep-o-Day Boys in battle. Following their victory, local Protestants formed the Orange Order which spread to many parts of Ulster.

The Order was modelled on the Freemasons and their oath went: 'I . . . do solemnly swear that I will, to the utmost of my power, support and defend the King and his heirs as long as he or they support the Protestant

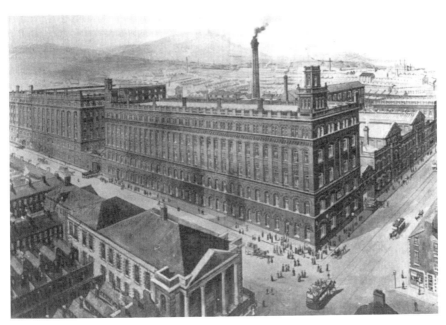

Thomas Gallaher's tobacco factory, York Street, Belfast, c. 1900, Ulster Museum.

ascendancy'. The Order's main aims were the protection of fellow-Protestants from Catholics, support for the Protestant religion and the maintenance of the monarchy and the constitution. Orangism spread to other countries thanks to emigration and military service, particularly to the USA, Canada, Australia, New Zealand and South Africa.

The Orange Lodges in Ireland are organised under the Grand Orange Lodge of Ireland, and within each county there is a Grand Lodge and subordinate lodges. There are surviving nineteenth-century directories of Orange Lodges in Ireland available at the Grand Lodge of Ireland:

- The 1856 directory gives lodge number, county, district, place the lodge met, post town, master's name and observations;

- The 1876 directory lists lodge number, master's name, county, district, sometimes place of meeting and post town, and observations;

- 'First and Second Reports from the Select Committee on Orange Lodges in Ireland with minutes of evidence and appendices 1835', Irish University Press Series of British Parliamentary Papers.

There is no centralised archive of Orange Order membership, and many records are still held with local lodges. Contact the Grand Orange Lodge of Ireland, which can research lodge numbers and forward requests to local lodges for information from their records. The contact details are:

Grand Orange Lodge of Ireland
65 Dublin Road
Belfast
BT2 7HE
Northern Ireland
Website: www.grandorange.org.uk/.

Hospital collections

PRONI also has in its custody records of various hospitals, reference HOS. Birth registers can be found in the hospital collections. These contain the date of birth of the infant, the name of the father and occupation and the mother's married and maiden name. It should be stressed, however, that these records are far from extensive and, like the Boards of Guardian records, are closed for 100 years from the latest date in the volume.

However, a search can be carried out to assist family/genealogical research, when the enquirer can show a close family connection with the subject of the enquiry in the closed section of the Board of Guardian and Hospital archives.

PRONI also has in its custody records of various mental hospitals. These include the minute books, account books, chaplains' books and committal papers of St Luke's Hospital, Armagh, 1824–c. 1956 (HOS/27/1). Also the records of Purdysburn Mental Hospital, County Down, comprising minute books, admission and discharge registers, daily state books, wages and salary books, reports and committal papers, 1829–c. 1950. The admission registers reflect progress in treatment of mental illness. In the 1830s conditions were diagnosed simply as 'mania', 'melancholia' or 'dementia'. These conditions might be ascribed to 'regret at not having any children', 'grief at husband going to America', 'religious excitement' or 'novel reading'. Behaviour that precipitated admission to hospital included a soldier's 'marching through the town of Antrim supposing he was in the company of Earl O'Neill' and a farmer 'supposing himself Mr O'Connell' (HOS/28/1).

Charity records

PRONI has in its custody a series of records relating to various charities that have operated in the Province during the past 200 years. These include the papers of various charities administered by the Commissioners of Charitable Donations and Bequests (see FIN/1). These contain the records of the Belfast Charitable Society, founded in 1752 to erect a poorhouse and hospital. PRONI has microfilmed some sixty volumes of the Society's records and these include Committee minutes, 1752–1955, Spring Water Commissioners' cash book, 1795–1805 and graveyard registers, 1797–1897 and these are available on microfilm reference MIC/61.

The Committee minutes contain a wealth of material that will be of interest to family and local historians. In July 1808, William Newsam, Orderly, recorded:

On Thursday I ordered a Coffin for a Child of the later Bell Man Irwin – that has been killed by a Cart in North Street – & on Friday a Coffin for an unfortunate Man that Hanged Himself in John Street – and on the same day I directed the admission to the Hospital of Willm. Leonard – an American Sailor – as will be seen by his Petition – I also directed the Readmission of Mary Cunningham who had run away from her apprenticeship, until the Committee would determine respecting her but I understand she has eloped from this also –

PRONI also holds the records of the Vaughan Charity, opened in 1787 with thirty boys of whom three were Roman Catholics. Girls were admitted to the benefit of the charity in 1828. The school was managed at long range by a board mostly of ecclesiastics, who rarely paid a visit. Its deposited records include a complete register of the male pupils from 1776 and a long series of minute books, 1823–1934. Reports were received and passed from chaplain, agent, schoolmaster, schoolmistress and medical officer. D/433.

Pedigrees

PRONI has in its custody records compiled by scholars that are of enormous interest to genealogists. Pedigrees for families from many different parts of Ireland are available. Most notable of these are extract pedigrees from wills proved in the Prerogative Court of Ireland between the sixteenth and eighteenth centuries compiled by or for Sir Bernard Burke, Ulster King of Arms. This collection of forty-two large volumes of Pedigree Charts is of great importance to all record searchers, T/559.

Also of interest are the Groves Manuscripts which contain a great deal of valuable material for genealogists. Tenison Groves, a Belfast genealogist and record searcher for more than forty years, compiled a collection of many thousands of transcripts, abstracts, notes, etc., which he made from records in the Public Record Office in Dublin before its partial destruction in 1922. That part of the collection which related to Northern Ireland was purchased by PRONI in 1939. The items, numbering over 9,000, include seventeenth-century muster rolls, militia lists and family pedigrees and are an invaluable source for genealogists. The Groves Manuscripts have been given the PRONI reference number T/808 and the catalogue, which features typescript extracts from these records, is available on the shelves of the Public Search Room.

Also of interest are:

- Ten volumes of transcripts of Irish genealogical material from the manuscript collections of the Society of Genealogists, London, 1569–1841, T/581;

- Canon Leslie's manuscripts, which include extracts from Armagh registry, clergy succession lists, extracts of about 700 wills and genealogical notes of numerous families, 1607–nineteenth century, T/1057;

- Extracts from Chancery and Exchequer bills, wills, etc., in the Public Record Office, Dublin, made by the Revd H B Swanzy, dealing mainly with the history of prominent families in counties Cavan, Fermanagh, Monaghan and Tyrone, c. 1620–1800, T/498.

Researchers should also consult the personal names index in the Public Search Room which contains many references to pedigrees and genealogical papers relating to various family names.

Ulster Covenant, 1912

The archive of the Ulster Unionist Council, held by PRONI, contains just under ½ million original signatures and addresses of the men who, on 28 September 1912, signed the Ulster Covenant, and of the women who signed the parallel Declaration. Previously the Covenant was difficult and very time-consuming to access and, consequently, it was under-used. PRONI has now improved access by digitising all the signatures, in recognition that the online database should make a significant contribution to both genealogical research and cultural tourism. The Ulster Covenant can be searched online at: www.proni.gov.uk/ulstercovenant/.

Sir Edward Carson signing the Covenant, PRONI.

APPENDIX

USEFUL ADDRESSES

Major repositories

* **Belfast Central Library**

Royal Avenue
Belfast
BT1 1EA
Northern Ireland
Telephone: (028) 9050 9150
Fax: (028) 9033 2819
Email: info@libraries.belfast-elb.gov.uk
Website: www.belb.org.uk

* **General Register Office, Belfast**

Northern Ireland Statistics and Research Agency
Oxford House
49/55 Chichester Street
Blefast
BT1 4HL
Northern Ireland
Telephone: (028) 9025 2000
Fax: (028) 9025 2044
Email: gro.nistra@dfpni.gov.uk (birth, death and marriage certificate
    enquiries)
Email: groreg.nistra@dfpni.gov.uk (marriage, re-registration and
    adoptions)
Email: grostats.nistra@dfpni.gov.uk (statistical queries)
Website: www.groni.gov.uk

- **Linen Hall Library**

17 Donegall Square
North Belfast
BT1 5GD
Northern Ireland
Telephone: (028) 9032 1707
Fax: (028) 9043 8586
Email: info@linenhall.com
Website: www.linenhall.com/Home/home.html

- **Public Record Office of Northern Ireland**

66 Balmoral Avenue
Belfast
BT9 6NY
Northern Ireland
Telephone: (028) 9025 5905
Fax: (028) 9025 5999
Email: proni@gov.uk
Website: proni.nics.gov.uk

- **Ulster American Folk Park**

Castletown
Omagh
County Tyrone
BT78 5QY
Northern Ireland
Telephone: (028) 8224 3292
Website: www.folkpark.com/

- **Ulster Folk and Transport Museum**

Cultra
Holywood
County Down
BT18 0EU
Northern Ireland
Telephone: (028) 9042 8428
Website: www.uftm.org.uk/

Heritage centres

- ## Armagh

Armagh Ancestry
42 English Street
Armagh
BT61 7AB
Northern Ireland
Telephone: (028) 3752 1802
Fax: (028) 3751 0033
Website: www.irishroots.net/Armagh.htm

- ## Londonderry/Derry

Heritage Library
14 Bishop Street
Derry City
County Londonderry
BT48 6PW
Northern Ireland
Telephone: (028) 7126 9792/7136 1661
Fax: (028) 7136 0921
Email: niancestors@btclick.com

- ## Banbridge Genealogy Services

c/o Banbridge Gateway Tourist Information Centre
200 Newry Road
Banbridge
County Down
BT32 3NB
Northern Ireland
Telephone: (028) 4062 6369
Fax: (028) 4062 3114
Website: www.banbridge.com

- ## Fermanagh/Tyrone

Heritage World
The Heritage Centre
26 Market Square
Dungannon

County Tyrone
BT70 1AB
Northern Ireland
Telephone: (028) 8772 4187
Fax: (028) 8775 2141
Website: www.irishroots.net/FnghTyrn.htm

• **Antrim/Down**

Ulster Historical Foundation
Balmoral Buildings
12 College Square East
Belfast
BTI 6DD
Northern Ireland
Telephone: (028) 9033 2288
Fax: (028) 9023 9885
Website: www.uhf.org.uk

Societies in Northern Ireland

• **North of Ireland Family History Society**

This Society, established in 1979, consists of ten family history societies in Northern Ireland and now has hundreds of members worldwide. The objective of the society is to foster an interest in family history with special reference to families who have roots in Northern Ireland. The Society publishes a journal, *North Irish Roots*, twice a year, providing a means for members to communicate their interests to others.

North of Ireland Family History Society
c/o Queen's University
Department of Education
Belfast
BT7 1HL
Northern Ireland
Website: www.nifhs.org

- **Presbyterian Historical Society**

Room 218
Church House
Fisherwick Place
Belfast
BT1 6DW
Northern Ireland
Telephone: (028) 9032 2284
Email: librarian@presbyterianhistoryireland.com
Website: www.presbyterianhistoryireland.com/

- **Baptist Union of Ireland**

117 Lisburn Road
Belfast
BT9 7AF
Northern Ireland

BIBLIOGRAPHY AND SOURCES

Adolph, Anthony, *Collins Tracing Your Irish Family History*, London, 2007

Bardon, Jonathan, *A History of Ulster*, Belfast, 1992

Begley, D F (ed.), *Irish Genealogy: A Record Finder*, Dublin, 1981

Carleton, S T, *Heads and Hearths: the Hearth Money Rolls and Poll Tax Returns for Co. Antrim, 1660–69*, Belfast, 1991

Clare, Revd W, *A Simple Guide to Irish Genealogy*, London, 1938

Connolly, S J (ed.), *The Oxford Companion To Irish History*, Oxford, 1998

Crawford, W H, 'The Ulster Irish in the Eighteenth Century', in *Ulster Folklife*, vol. 28, 1982

Crawford, W H, 'The Significance of Landed Estates in Ulster 1600–1820', in *Irish Economic and Social History*, XVII, 1990

Crawford, W H and Trainor, B, *Aspects of Irish Social History, 1750–1800*, Belfast, 1969

De Breffny, Brian, *Irish Family Names: Arms, Origins and Locations*, Dublin, 1982

Dickson, R J, *Ulster Emigration To Colonial America, 1718–1775*, Belfast, 1966

Fabricant, Carol, *Swift's Landscape*, London, 1982

Falley, M D, *Irish and Scotch-Irish Ancestral Research*, Virginia, 1962

Gillespie, R G (ed.), *Settlement And Survival On An Ulster Estate*, Belfast, 1988

Gillespie, R G and O'Sullivan, Harold (eds), *The Borderlands: Essays On The History of the Ulster-Leinster Border*, Belfast, 1989

Green, E R R (ed.), *Essays in Scotch-Irish History*, Belfast, 1969

Grenham, J, *Tracing Your Irish Ancestors*, Dublin, 1992

Hayward, Richard, *In Praise of Ulster*, Belfast, 1938

Herber, Mark D, *Ancestral Trails: The Complete Guide To British Genealogy and Family History*, Stroud, 1997

Hey, David, *The Oxford Companion to Local And Family History*, Oxford, 1996

Johnston, Jack (ed.), *Workhouses of the North West*, County Fermanagh, 1996

Kinealy, Christine, *Tracing Your Irish Roots*, Belfast, 1991

Kinealy, Christine and Parkhill, Trevor (eds), *The Famine In Ulster*, Belfast, 1997

Lucey, M, 'Rateable Valuation in Ireland', in *Administration*, Spring 1964, vol. 12, no. 1

MacAtasney, G, *Famine In Lurgan and Portadown*, Dublin, 1997

McCarthy, T, *The Irish Roots Guide*, Dublin, 1991

MacConghail, Maire and Gorry, Paul, *Tracing Your Irish Ancestors*, Glasgow, 1997

MacCuarta, Brian (ed.), *Ulster 1641: Aspects of the Rising*, Belfast, 1993

MacLysaght, E, *Irish Families: Their Names, Arms and Origins*, Dublin, 1957

MacLysaght, E, 'Seventeenth Century Hearth Money Rolls', in *Analecta Hibernica*, no. 24

Maxwell, I, *Tracing Your Ancestors In Northern Ireland*, Edinburgh, 1997

Maxwell, I, *Tracing Armagh Ancestors*, Belfast, 2000

Maxwell, I, *Tracing Down Ancestors*, Belfast, 2004

Maxwell, I, *How To Trace Your Irish Ancestors*, Oxford, 2008

Maxwell, I, *Your Irish Ancestors: A Guide to the Family Historian*, Barnsley, 2008

Neill, K, *How To Trace Family History In Northern Ireland*, Belfast, 1986

Nolan, W, *Tracing the Past*, Dublin, 1982

Nolan, W (ed.), *The Shaping of Ireland: The Geographical Perspective*, Dublin, 1986

O'Neill, Robert K, *Ulster Libraries: A Visitors Guide*, Belfast, 1987

Ouimette, David S, *Finding Your Irish Ancestors: A Beginners Guide*, Salt Lake City, 2005

Phair, P B, 'Guide to the Registry of Deeds', in *Hibernica Analecta*, no. 3

Quinn, S E, *Trace Your Irish Ancestors*, Wicklow, 1989

Robinson, Philip, *The Plantation of Ulster*, Belfast, 1994

Roulston, William, *Researching Scots-Irish Ancestors: the Essential Guide to Early Modern Ulster, 1600–1800*, Belfast, 2005

Ryan, J G, *Irish Church Records*, Dublin, 1992

Vaughan, W E, *Landlords & Tenants in Mid-Victorian Ireland*, Oxford, 1994

Walker, B M, *Ulster Politics: The Formative Years, 1868–86*, Belfast, 1989

INDEX

adoption, 28
almanacs, 113
Alphabetical Index to the Townlands and Towns, Parishes and Baronies of Ireland, 90
Anglican Church, 59–61
Anglo-Normans, 2–3
Armagh, 2, 59
Armagh 'census', 1770, 32
Army records, 138–40
attainted, 48–49
Aughrim, battle of 50
Australia, 159

Baptist Church records, 72
Belfast, 4–10, 63–65
Belfast Academy, 84
Belfast Central Library, 16–17
Belfast Charitable Society, 169
Belfast Corporation, 60, 130–31
Belfast News-Letter, 121
Belfast and Province of Ulster Directory, 115
Belfast Special Constabulary, 153–54
Betham, Sir William, 108
birth certificates, 26
Board of Guardian records, *see* Irish Poor Law
Books of Survey and Distribution, 41–42
Boru, Brian, 59
Boyne, battle of, 50
business records, 165–66

calendars of patent rolls, 37
Campbell College, 84

Canada, 158
Catholic Church, 62–63, 68–69, 110
Catholic migrants from Ulster, 1795–96, 34
Catholic Relief Act, 1829, 148
Celts, 1–2
'Census' of 1659, 43–44
'Census of Fews', 36
census records, 20–23
  1813, 20
  1821, 20
  1831–34, 20
  1841, 21
  1851, 21
  1861–91, 22
  1901, 22–23
  1911, 23
census substitutes,
  1659, 43
  1740, 31
  1766, 31
Charles I, 37
charter schools, 79
charity records, 169–70
Chichester, Sir Arthur, 4–5, 51
Church of Ireland, 60–61, 65–67
Church of the Latter-Day Saints, 29
Church records, 59–77
  Baptist, 72
  census, 75–76
  Church of Ireland, 65–67
  Congregational, 71–72
  Huguenot, 74
  indexes, 67–68
  Jewish, 74–75
  Methodist, 70
  Moravian, 73

Non-Subscribing Presbyterian, 72–73
Presbyterian, 69–70
Reformed Presbyterian, 73
Religious Society of Friends, 71–72
Roman Catholic, 68–69
Church Temporalities, 103
civil registration, 25–29
Civil Survey, 42
Congregational Church, 71
Consistorial Courts, 108
corporations, 130–33
cotton industry, 7
County Constabulary, 152
county councils, 136
court-leet, 97
court records, 154–56
Cromwell, Oliver, 5, 40–43
Cromwellian settlement, 42–43
Crown and Peace records, 154–57
Cuchullain, 2

death certificates, 27
depositions of 1641, 40–42
Diamond, battle of 167
directories
    countrywide, 114
    provincial, 115–19
District Electoral Divisions, 22–23
DNA, 18–19

education
    national schools, 80–83
    secondary, 84
    university, 85
election records, 147–50
electoral registers, 149–50
Elizabeth I, 3
Emancipation Act (1829), 147
emigration records, 157–63
encumbered estates records, 105–6
evictions, 100

family history centres, 17
fiants of the Tudor sovereigns, 36–37
Flaxseed Premiums, 1796, 33–34
'Flight of the Earls', 3, 51
Franciscan Petition Lists, 1670–71, 47–48
freeholders, 147–50

Genealogical Office, 108
General Register Office, Belfast, 27–29
Gerald of Wales, 2
Glorious Revolution, 45, 49
grammar schools, 82
Grand Juries, 134–36
gravestone inscriptions, 18, 24
Great Famine, 123–26
Griffith's Valuation, 89–91
Groves, Tenison, 31, 170
Guide to Records of the Irish Society and the London Companies, 58

Hall, Mr and Mrs, 78, 80–81, 165–66
Harland and Wolff, 166
hearth-money rolls, 45–46
hedge schools, 79
heritage centres, 17–18
Home Rule, 8
hospital records, 168–69
Householders' Index, 92
Householders Returns, 1766, 31–32
Huguenot records, 74
Huguenot Society, 74

indexes
    births, marriages and deaths, 27–29
    prerogative wills, 108–9
    wills, 109
International Genealogical Index, 17
Irish Genealogical Project, 12
Irish Land Commission, 101–3
Irish Society, 56–57

James I, 51–52, 54
James II, 48–50

Jewish records, 74–75

Kildare Place Society, 80

Land Registry, 101–2
landed estate records, 93–106
law and order, 152–56
leases, 99
libraries, 17
Linen Hall Library, Belfast, 16
linen industry, 7, 33
local-government records, 130–36
London Companies, 54, 56–57
   records, 56–57
Londonderry, 49

marriage certificates, 26–27
Marriage Licence Bonds, 76–77
Married Women's Property Act,
   1882, 107
Martin's Belfast Directory, 115
Methodist Church records, 70
Methodist College, 84
military records, 138–46
militia records, 141–43
Moravian Church, 73
muster rolls, 37–40

national schools, 80–83
Navan Fort, 2
newspapers, 119–21
Newsplan, 121
Non-Subscribing Presbyterian
   Church, 72–73
North of Ireland Family History
   Society, 18

O'Connell, Daniel, 80, 147
O'Neill, Hugh, Earl of Tyrone, 3, 51
O'Neill, Sir Turlough McHenry, 36
old-age pension claims, 24
Orange Order records, 166–68
Ordnance Survey maps, 91
Ordnance Survey Memoirs, 112–13

passenger lists, 160–62
pedigrees, 170–71
Penal Laws, 62–63, 79
Pigot's Commercial Directory of Ireland,
   114
Plantation of Ulster, 2–4, 51–58
   survey, 1611, 55
   survey, 1613, 55
   survey, 1618–19, 55
   survey, 1622, 55
police records, 152–54
poll books, 148–50
Poll Tax returns, 1660s, 44–45
Poor Law records, 122–28
Poor Law Union, 122
Prerogative Court of Armagh, 108
Presbyterian Church, 61–62
Presbyterian Historical Society, 74
Primary Valuation of Ireland (Griffith),
   89–91
printed sources, 112–21
Protestant householders, 1740, 31
Public Record Office of Northern
   Ireland, 15–16, 159
Pynnar, Nicholas, 4

Quaker records, 71
Queen's University, 85–86

rebellion, 1798, 34
Reformed Presbyterian Church
   records, 73
Register of Trees, 155–56
Registry of Deeds, 103–5
Religious Society of Friends, 71
rentals, 98
Report on Fictitious Votes, 155–56
Return of Owners of Land . . . 98
Revaluation of Belfast, 92
rising, 1641, 5
Royal Belfast Academical Institution,
   85
Royal Inniskillen Fusiliers Museum
   140

Royal Irish Constabulary, 152–53
Royal Irish Fusiliers, 138–40
Royal Irish Rifles, 140

St Patrick, 1–2, 59
school records, 78–85
  registers, 83
Scottish settlement, 52–55
Second World War, 9
Siege of Derry, 49–50
Slater's *Directory of Ireland*, 114
societies, 18
solicitors' collections, 164–65
spirit licence registers, 155
Statistical Survey of County Tyrone, 81
stock returns, 1803, 100
street directories, 113
subsidy rolls, 46–47
surnames, 12–15
Survey of Downpatrick, 31

tenant farmers, 95
Test Act, 61
testamentary records, 107–11
Thackeray, William Makepeace, 7, 64
*Thom's Irish Almanac and Official
  Directory*, 114
Titanic, 166
tithe applotment books, 87–88
tithe system, 87–88
title deeds, 99
town book of the Corporation of Belfast,
  131
Town Commissioners, 133–34

townland valuation, 1830s, 89
Treaty of Limerick, 62

Ulster American Folk Park, 162–63
Ulster Covenant, 1912, 171
Ulster Custom, 95
Ulster Volunteer Force, 8–9
undertakers, 53
United Irishmen, 34–35
University Calendars, 85–86

valuation records, 87–92
  first general valuation, 89–90
  townland valuation, 89
valuation revisions, 91–92
Vaughan Charity, 170
vestry records, 66–67
Volunteer records, 145–46
voters lists, 149

Welsh settlement, 54
Wesley, John, 70
Wilde, Oscar, 82
William III, 49–50
wills and testamentary records,
  107–11
  before 1858, 108–9
  1858–1900, 109–10
  1900–, 110–11
workhouses, 122–27
Wyndam Act, 96

Yeomanry records, 143–45